M000077548

HUSTLE

HUSTLE

THE LIFE CHANGING EFFECTS OF CONSTANT
MOTION

JESSE WARREN TEVELOW

OCEAN PARK PRESS

This book is uncopyrighted. It was made possible by readers like you. Feel free to re-publish, re-tool, and otherwise share its contents as you see fit.

Limit of Liability / Disclaimer of Warranty: While the author has put forth his best effort to present true and correct information throughout this book, he makes no representations or warranties with respect to the accuracy or completeness of its contents. The advice and strategies contained herein may not be suitable for your situation. You should consult with a professional where appropriate. The author is not liable for any loss of profit or any other commercial damages, including but not limited to special, incidental, or consequential damages.

The author is not responsible for websites (or their content) that are not owned by the author.

Hustle/ Jesse Warren Tevelow

First Edition: 2015
Printed in the United States of America

1. Lifestyle. 2. Quality of work life. 3. Quality of life. 4. Business. I. Title: Hustle

ISBN 978-0692601228

Book design and illustrations by Jesse Warren Tevelow
Cover design by Jesse Warren Tevelow
Photography by PJ Russ

Bonus Gift: Get My Next Book for Free

My very first book, *The Connection Algorithm*, was self-published. It's now a #1 bestseller on track to generate $20,000 per year in passive income. Other part-time authors are doing far better than me, earning six, or even seven figures per year. Here's the best part: We're not writing because we have to. *We're writing because we want to.* This wasn't possible ten years ago, but the publishing industry has changed. People are finding unparalleled freedom and wealth through writing, and you can too. My forthcoming book, *The Dawn of Books*, will show you how.

If you've ever dreamt of using your knowledge for more than just a paycheck, *The Dawn of Books* is for you. And you're in luck, because you can reserve a pre-release copy **at no cost** by visiting www.jtev.me and joining my mailing list. It's honestly that simple. No strings attached.

The Dawn of Books will change the way you think about writing, but it will also prepare you to thrive in the entrepreneurial era we find ourselves in (even if you don't want to become a fulltime author). To give you unparalleled insight into the world of publishing and entrepreneurship, I've spent the past year conducting in-depth interviews with some of the industry's best and brightest. Here's a sampling:

- **Brad Feld** Author of the Startup Revolution series, managing director of Foundry Group (over \$1 billion under management).
- **Taylor Pearson** Amazon #1 bestselling author of The End of Jobs.
- **Rob Walling** Founder and CEO of Drip, serial entrepreneur, author, podcaster.
- **Rohit Bhargava** Wallstreet Journal bestselling author of five business books, founder of Influential Marketing Group.
- **Chandler Bolt** 21 year old entrepreneur, running a seven-figure business for self-publishing. Author of five bestselling books on Amazon.
- **Simon Whistler** Creator of Rocking-Self Publishing, a popular podcast that explores the world of self-published books.

...just to name a few.

Are you curious about the benefits of writing a book, but too overwhelmed to get started? I can relate. I made plenty of poor choices with my first book, and wasted thousands of dollars. *The Dawn of Books* demystifies the process so you can avoid those same mistakes.

Inside, you'll find various tools and techniques you can use to guarantee a polished manuscript, a timely launch, and maximized profits (without the headaches). It's jam-packed with field-tested resources, including the email template I used to secure an endorsement from Tony Horton, detailed production timelines, guidelines for crafting a winning outline, software recommendations, tips for creating a professional design on a budget, and much more.

To reserve a free copy of *The Dawn of Books*, just go to www.jtev.me and join my mailing list. I've poured a lot of energy into this, and I know you're going to love it!

Cheers,

—J

CONTENTS

For my father, who taught me the power of passion, persistence, and positivity.

"Be not afraid of going slowly. Be afraid only of standing still."

–CHINESE PROVERB

CHAPTER 1

INTRODUCTION

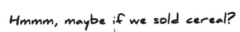

Brian Chesky is the founder of Airbnb, a multi-billion dollar company. But it wasn't always worth that much. In fact, the company struggled to pay its bills for years before hitting its stride. At one point, Brian was selling branded cereal boxes as a way to make extra cash. Seriously. Cereal. He turned the experience into a cultural lesson, explaining to his employees that the company was built by Cereal Entrepreneurs (a wordplay on the common expression "serial entrepreneur").[1]

Sometimes you have to get creative to make ends meet, or to reach the next rung on the ladder, or to escape the quicksand. That's called *hustling*.

Hustling is also about bending the rules. Before Jamie Foxx was Jamie Foxx, he was Eric Marlon Bishop. He would go to comedy shows and sign up to go on stage and perform. Each night, the manager would call out the names of amateur comedians who would perform that night. Eric (Jamie) was talented. After his first performance, he got a standing ovation. But then he ran into a problem. The manager stopped calling his name! He wasn't sure why this happened, but he was determined to get back up on stage—by any means necessary.

After a while, he noticed the manager would always call at least one girl's name. There weren't many female performers at that time, and it seemed the manager wanted to give them a fighting chance. So, Eric started putting down fake androgynous names on the list. Pat, Kelly, Erin...Jamie. One night, it finally worked. They called his name. He

---

[1] http://tinyurl.com/qdmmnha

got back up on stage, and got a second standing ovation.

Not only that, but when people called out his name to congratulate him, he didn't respond, making him seem cocky. Of course in reality, Jamie just didn't identify as *Jamie* yet. But it worked in his favor. People began to think he had swagger—a certain "it" factor that made him talented. His budding career was on track again, mainly because he bent the rules. *Because he hustled.*

Hustling is also about grinding. It's about doing whatever it takes. Tony Horton is arguably the most famous fitness expert in the world. He is the creator of P90X, one of the most popular workout programs ever put on DVD. Tony has trained a seemingly endless list of celebrities, including Tom Petty, Annie Lennox, and Usher—to name a few. But he didn't just walk up to these celebrities and start demanding pushups. He had to hustle through some muck first.

Tony began his career as an aspiring actor. He wanted to be in Hollywood. So he moved to LA, without any money—or a plan. He kept auditioning for gigs, but wasn't landing any roles. Tony was, admittedly, a little fat and overweight. He thought, *"Maybe if I workout and get fit, I'll get chosen."*

After finding success in the gym, fitness eventually took center stage and became his full-time career. Slowly but surely, he built up a client base. When he landed a few celebrity clients, his reputation took off, which elevated his notoriety and ultimately led to P90X. But what many people don't know is that Tony also performed as a mime on the Santa Monica pier while developing his clout as a fitness expert. He wasn't earning enough money at first, so he had to somehow make ends meet.

On his earlier quest to become an actor, he had learned how to mime. To pay the bills, he'd go down to the pier nearly every day, acting out provocative scenarios (like picking up a girl at a bar, for example) in full mime makeup and attire. It was how he bridged the gap. He hustled hard.

If *you* happen to be hustling, you might find yourself doing a job on the side, or working on a non-traditional project, or freelancing, or temping for an unknown company, or veering off from your main goal in some way. While it can feel like an admission of failure, it's not. It's what I call an in-between moment. The best hustlers hustle all the time. Whether they're in the valley or atop the mountain, they're hustling. If you want to get anywhere worthwhile, there's no other choice.

There's a difference between hustling and settling. Settling is admitting defeat and abandoning the bigger picture. It's when the passion dies, and the fire goes out for good. Hustling is simply taking the next step, whatever that might be. It's about not standing still. Making moves.

If you keep hustling, amazing things will happen—eventually. This little book is meant to gently push you into the next step. And the next. And the next. Until something incredible happens.

Here's one of my secrets to getting through the tougher times: Hustling during the in-between moments can lead to epiphanies that will alter the course of your existence for the better. The act of the hustle is more important than whatever it is you're doing, or wherever it is you're planning to go. *Constant motion delivers life-changing results.* So focus on the constant motion part, not the destination part.

My last book was a #1 bestseller. It took a year to produce. This book is different. I wrote it, edited it, and published it in seven days. That's right, seven. Why? Because it was a hustle project—and a bit of an experiment. Honestly, I really needed the money. But I also wanted to prove a point to myself: Hustling is powerful. More specifically, building momentum can lead to unthinkable results. Sometimes you *have* to hustle. You have to make something happen.

THE POWER OF MOMENTUM

"Every day I'm hustlin'" —*Rick Ross*

The common thread in the stories I just told you about is that Brian, Tony, and Jamie didn't give up. They kept going. They kept moving. By continually moving, they eventually broke through their barriers and gained momentum. We all know that momentum helps. That's easy to comprehend. It makes logical sense. But let's take a moment to understand exactly *why* it's so incredibly powerful.

What creates momentum? *Movement.* When you take action and put things out into the world, stuff happens. Eventually, there are results. The more you move, and the quicker you move, the more results you get. When you get results, it leads to inspiration and motivation, which then leads back to momentum. In other words, the cycle feeds on itself. This is why constant motion is the crucial, core characteristic of every hustler.

Motivation

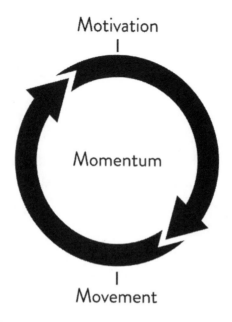

Momentum

Movement

While stepping forward is profoundly empowering, standing still is equally catastrophic. (Take a moment to digest that). That's true because the cycle also occurs in reverse. When you stop moving, you lose feedback, which saps inspiration and motivation. If you lose motivation, you lose momentum. And when you're in that state, you can't make progress toward your personal growth. Once that happens, things only get harder and the situation continues to worsen.

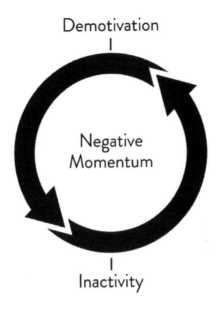

Demotivation

Negative
Momentum

Inactivity

This is when you find yourself back in ZombieLand, at a 9-5 job with zero motivation. Or worse, laying in bed, horribly depressed, with no desire to get up. When you stand still, you're actually moving *backwards*, because it becomes incredibly difficult to gain momentum once it's lost. This is why simply stepping forward day after day, making *some* progress, and practicing even the tiniest bit of hustle is so critical to your happiness, growth, and overall success.

You don't need to be constantly sprinting as fast as you can toward a finish line you'll never reach. Of course, if you do that, you'll burn out. You just need to have a goal—some kind of purpose. This will undoubtedly require plenty of work, but also breaks. Maybe even extended vacations. The cycle only reverses when you have *nothing* in the works, and you've lost all sense of forward motion.

> *"Mine is a pretty simple strategy: There's not a lot of talent here, but there's a lot of hustle. I have to be in every place I can, and be busy." —Ryan Seacrest*

The power of momentum is the secret weapon used by all hustlers to achieve incredible success. They understand that it affects their ability to prevail, more so than intellect, money, or even talent.

And here's the best part: Momentum is easiest to gain when you have nothing to lose. When your back is against the wall, and failure doesn't matter, you don't have to be careful. You can be daring and move as quickly as you want. When you move at great speeds, momentum naturally accelerates.

In physics, force is a function of mass and acceleration. ($f = m * a$). The same applies to life in general. If you gain momentum by working quickly, and then put a lot of focus (i.e. mass) behind whatever it is you're doing, it will generate tremendous force—which usually leads to positive results. So hustling, whether fast or slow, isn't just a smart thing to do every once in awhile—it's a smart way to *live*.

WHO THIS BOOK IS FOR

This book is for doubters.
If you think hustling is dumb, give this book a chance. You might be surprised at how important hustling can be. Maybe you think hard work is more important than hustling. But hustling *is* hard work. Maybe you think grinding is more important than finding shortcuts. Well, hustling is actually both. A hustler isn't a swindler. A hustler is simply a doer. Open your mind, and you'll see there's a hustler in all of us. Even *you*.

There are common misconceptions about what it takes to hustle, what it means, and how to do it well. If you dread the thought of hustling, consider these simple truths:

- Making a project, task, or piece of content shorter and simpler makes it more palatable, and therefore more useful.
- Planning is easier, and more accurate, when there is less to plan.
- Thinking and solving problems is easier when you're thinking about less.

This isn't to say that hustling is easy, or that all projects are simple. That's certainly not the case. But hustling also isn't as horrible or overwhelming as you might think.

This book is for dreamers.

If you're stuck in a rut and looking for more out of life, hustling might hold the answer. It could be the spark that snaps you out of your boring routine and gives you something to work toward. If you're a dreamer, my goal is to turn you into a doer.

There's never been a better time to hustle. Since the very beginning of our existence, people have been hustling. Sadly, over the past few hundred years, we've grown lazy. We've become entitled. To make matters worse, the life we've come to expect is no longer being handed to us on a silver platter. Technology and globalization, paired with an unstable economy, have made that lifestyle far from guaranteed. Hustling is now more important than ever. It's quickly becoming our only means of survival.

This book is for doers.

If you're already hustling, this book will help you through it. As you know, hustling is tough. The challenges you face will never be black and white. Sometimes it will feel like you aren't getting anywhere, but you are. You just have to keep making moves.

This book is also meant to be a practical toolkit. You'll find some old tricks, and hopefully some new ones to help you along your journey.

A common problem with hustlers (myself included) is that we often forget what we're fighting for. Just as a lazy person can become blinded by his complacency, a hustler can become blinded by his incessant drive. This book invites you to pause for a moment—to force you to ask yourself, *"Why am I really doing this?"*

When you stop and think about why you do what you do, it provides context. This context then creates clarity, which leads to better decision-making, and finally unparalleled momentum. So put your hustle on hold for a minute. Let's examine why we hustle in the first place.

YOU HAVE TWO OPTIONS

1. Easy and boring.
2. Hard and exciting.

Which do you choose? If you're lazy, you'll choose #1. But it depends on what we're talking about, doesn't it? Stuffing envelopes is easy and boring. Climbing a mountain is hard and exciting. Now which do you choose? Still #1? We need more information. For example, how many envelopes do you have to stuff? And how tall is the mountain? Let's look at this from an extreme perspective. You can either:

1. Stuff envelopes for the rest of your life
2. Climb mountains for the rest of your life

Most people will now choose #2. Why? Because I added the phrase: *for the rest of your life*. You only have one life to live. If you were to fill that life with one activity, of course most people would opt for an activity that's exciting, even if it's hard. Who wants to stuff envelopes until they die?

The amazing thing about this exercise is that even though most people pick #2, they realize they've actually chosen #1 when mapping the two options to real life. Any one of us could choose to climb mountains for a living, versus stuffing envelopes. But how many of us are actually mountain climbers? The reason we choose envelopes over mountains in real life is because the envelopes are easier and safer. Isn't that sad? This is your *life* we're talking about.

If you just realized you're selling yourself short, and then had a mini panic attack, you're not alone. A frighteningly large percentage of the world is just pushing papers around—stuffing envelopes. My goal is to break you free from that—to teach you how to climb.

UP AND DOWN

I've had millions of dollars tied to my net worth in the form of stock. Then it all disappeared. I've had over six digits in liquid cash sitting in my personal bank account, and seen it fade away to nothing. Throughout my entire adult life, I've cycled between doing work to pay the bills, doing work for some kind of recognition (a big payday, or social status), and doing work I care about. After experiencing all three, I can tell you that doing work you care about is worth losing all the money in the world.

Yes, you have to pay the bills. That's a given. And that's where life gets hard. But in my experience, as long as you keep a little hustle in your day—you can survive both from a food-and-shelter standpoint, *and* a sense-of-worth standpoint. Do you want to be a hustler? I hope so. Take a deep breath and buckle up. It's a wild ride.

CHAPTER 2

WHERE DOES HUSTLE COME FROM?

Hustle comes from confidence, an aversion to settling, and a desire to work hard. But where do THOSE things come from? While the answers might be obvious, we typically don't take the time to internalize them. Pretend, for a moment, that you just stepped into this world for the first time.

You don't know anything about how it works, how you're supposed to feel, or who else is in it. Let your worries and doubts fade away. Your mind is a blank canvas, ready for fresh paint.

CONFIDENCE

For hustle to exist, you need confidence. Confidence is a choice. Let me say that again: *Confidence is a choice*. Want confidence? It's yours. Take it. It's that simple. People ask me all the time where my confidence comes from. I tell them I have no idea. Let me be honest with you: My confidence lapses all the time. I become extremely doubtful when I'm pushing my limits particularly hard. But that's when I know I'm on to something. When I feel the self-doubt creeping in, I relax, which we'll talk about later.

Confidence doesn't come with experience, it's enhanced by experience. Confidence comes from deep inside you. Here's a painfully obvious trick that most people fail to employ: Surround yourself with people who support you, and deliberately disengage with people who doubt you. I don't care if it's your best friend, your mother, or your boss. If they're constantly feeding you words of doubt—get away. Your ability to reach your full potential will skyrocket as soon as you remove external haters. As Taylor Swift says, "haters gonna' hate." That's because they're jealous or scared. And you don't want to be either of those things, do you?

AN AVERSION TO SETTLING

Some of us just don't feel comfortable with the status quo. If sitting around at night watching TV makes your brain boil, you're probably a hustler. If you can't bare the thought of being a cog in a wheel, you're probably a hustler. If you want random people to know your name and what you stand for, you're probably a hustler. It's not about being famous or rich or powerful. It's about making a difference in the world—doing something that matters.

Be careful how you interpret what I just said. The examples above are not all-encompassing—not even close. They're simply common indicators. Being a hustler does not preclude you from working at a big corporation, or working between the hours of 9-5, or being a stay-at-home parent (...or even watching TV). Droves of bonafide hustlers are operating in *all* of those situations.

Hustling is a behavioral trait, not a societal circumstance. You can be clocking in at 9 and clocking out at 5, and still be hustling at one of the most in-spired organizations in the world. Basecamp and Supercell are two such companies that instantly come to mind. (Look them up. You might want to get involved.) Or, you could be clocking in at 9 and clocking out at 5, staring at the wall the entire day and hating your life. The difference between those two scenarios is your internal mentality and drive—not the corporate structure. The corporate structure is just a container for your experience.

What this means is that you have to track your mood. Only you can define *settling* for yourself. It's different for everyone. Do you like what you're do-ing, or not? Are you invigorated throughout your day? Are you waking up happy and excited, or with dread? The traditional labels of who you are, what you do, or where you fit in society don't matter. What matters is how you feel.

Settling, just like hustling, is defined by your mental state. They're on opposite ends of the spec-trum. Where do you fall on that line?

A DESIRE TO WORK HARD

"Talent is cheaper than table salt. What sep-arates the talented individual from the

successful one is a lot of hard work."
—Stephen King

Why do some of us work hard and some of us sit on our asses all day? Dan Pink, a New York Times and Wallstreet Journal bestselling author, argues that there are three main motivators—and they're not what you think. Money doesn't make the list. In fact, money can be a demotivator. It turns out that once you get beyond work that only requires rudimentary cognitive skill, higher monetary rewards are inversely related to performance. Instead, emotion becomes the driving force. More specifically, Pink defines the three main motivators as autonomy, mastery, and purpose.[2] This has been backed up by numerous scientific studies. Here's one:

"Psychologists Teresa Amabile and Steven Kramer interviewed over 600 managers and found a shocking result. 95 percent of managers misunderstood what motivates employees. They thought what motivates employees was making money, getting raises and bonuses. In fact, after analyzing over 12,000 employee diary entries, they discovered that the number one work motivator

---

[2] https://youtu.be/Y64ms-htffE

was emotion, not financial incentive: It's the feeling of making progress every day toward a meaningful goal."[3]

Consider what this means. If you aren't hardworking, maybe it's not because you're lazy, but because you hate what you're working on! I believe there's a hustler in all of us. It isn't about your genetic makeup. It's about your environment and the emotional state in which you're operating. If you're having trouble getting up in the morning and going to work, there's a good chance you'd be happier hustling. You just need to find the right thing to be hustling toward, and the right people to support you. If you had all the free time in the world, what would you want to master? What would give you a sense of purpose? What would make your heart beat a little louder? The hustle is somewhere inside you. You just have to find it and set it free.

---

[3] http://tinyurl.com/pr7wt3a

CHAPTER 3

HUSTLER'S DIARY- DAY 1

This book is an experiment. I wanted to see if I could write and launch a full book in seven days. In an effort to make that happen—and give you a glimpse into the process, I decided to keep journal entries as I was writing. Here's the first entry:

Wednesday, December 9th, 2015

7:30 a.m. I'm feeling miserable this morning. I'm working on a big book project. It's about the self-publishing industry. I've been interviewing high-profile experts to gain more insight, which has been great. The problem? I'm low on cash. The book still needs a lot of work. It probably won't launch for another several months. I need a way to keep this project going. I need to bridge the gap.

8 a.m. I have a crazy idea. What if I write a second book using the opposite approach, as a way to quickly infuse more cash into the initial project? Meaning, what if I write a book as fast as I possibly can? Instead of spending a year or more on it, I'll aim to write it in three days, and publish it in seven. No interviews with experts. No endorsements. No editors, book designers, or marketing managers. I'll just use everything I've learned and put out the best product I can, in the shortest time possible. This will *hopefully* do two things:

1. *Generate extra income so I can keep pursuing my initial book project.*
2. *Serve as valuable research material. After all, there are various approaches to writing a book. I haven't tried the 'quick and dirty' approach. Now is as good a time as ever.*

Writing a book in three days sounds ludicrous, I know. But it's possible. I'm not planning on writing a long book. It'll be short. 100-150 pages at most. If I can write 10,000 words per day, I'll have 30,000 words, which puts me in the range I want. I know this will take extreme focus, but I'm ready for it. I thrive on extreme focus (most people do). As Gary Keller, author of The One Thing, teaches: We should always be asking, "What's the one thing I can do this week such that by doing it, everything else would be easier or unnecessary?" This is my one thing for the next seven days. Let's do it.

5 p.m. I've written 8,000 words. Almost there. I also had a great idea: I could capture my experience with journal entries. I included journal entries in my last book, The Connection Algorithm, and they were a huge hit. Why not do it again? That's what hustler's do: Find what works, and repeat. In case you're wondering, no...I didn't write the stuff above in real time. I had to go back and do it from memory once I decided I would be writing journal entries. I cheated. That's another thing hustlers do. We break the rules, when necessary ;) Shhh, don't tell.

8 p.m 10,000 words. Done. I cheated again. I went back through my old blog posts and found some material that related to this book. After a bit of editing, they fit right in. I maintained a pace of about 1,000 words per hour today. Even though I've worked a solid 13 hours, I'm feeling energized. Two more days and I'm done. Holy shit, this is starting to feel strangely possible.

WHAT DOES HUSTLE REQUIRE?

Hustling requires a different mindset than most people have. It's ideal if you're just naturally geared to be that way. But if not, don't worry. It can certainly be learned. In my experience, the best way to achieve such a mentality is to surround yourself with people who already have it. For some of us, that's our parents. For others, you'll have to fly further from the nest. If after reading this section, no one comes to mind, let this book be your first hustler companion. But you should find real people, too. People make better friends than books.

FINDING THE JOY IN FEAR

Every so often, the fears and doubts of my younger self echo in my head. When I entertain those thoughts, I realize how nervous I was back then. It was a horrible way to live. When I was in the process of writing my first book, my younger-self was especially bothersome, often yapping in my ear as I tried to work. Eventually, I decided to settle things for good. Here's the conversation I had (yes, with myself).

Younger Me: Got a minute? I'm concerned. I need to get some things off my chest.

Me: Sure, what's up?

YM: I'm in deep trouble. I'm really stressed.

M: What are you stressed about?

YM: Well, I'm working on building a company. It's completely new to me. I don't know if I'm doing things the right way or not. It's really difficult, and there's a good chance I'm going to fail.

M: I understand. That can be stressful.

YM: Do things ever get better? What's your life like right now?

M: Well, I'm working on writing a book. It's completely new to me. I don't know if I'm doing things the right way or not. It's really difficult, and there's a good chance I'm going to fail.

YM: Sounds like you can relate to me. So, are you stressed? Are you losing sleep at night? Are you upset you decided to write the book in the first place?

M: Actually, I'm not stressed at all. I get plenty of sleep, and I'm definitely glad I decided to write the book. It's invigorating.

YM: I don't get it. How do you live in constant uncertainty without it turning into fear?

M: Have you ever been to an amusement park?

YM: Yes.

M: Have you ever ridden on a roller coaster?

YM: Yes.

M: When you ride a roller coaster, is it scary to you?

YM: Yes—but it's also fun.

M: Exactly. And do you ever worry you'll fly off the tracks?

YM: No.

M: Precisely.

YM: I don't get it.

M: Life is an amusement park. Fear happens to be one of the best ways for us to feel alive. There's immense joy in that. Do you really want to be the person who never rides the roller coaster?

YM: I guess not. That would be pretty sad.

M: Yes, it would. So, here's what you need to do: Ride the roller coaster. When you feel the fear, let it remind you how alive you are. Enjoy the excitement of it. Trust that you aren't going to fly off the tracks.

YM: I think I understand.

M: Good, because at some point, your trip to the amusement park will end. And you'll feel like an idiot if you spent the whole time complaining instead of enjoying the ride.

RISK TOLERANCE: ARE YOU A TURKEY OR A CHEETAH?

As the last section suggests, you need to have a healthy risk tolerance if you plan on hustling. Just keep in mind, almost everything is risky these days. In *The End of Jobs*, Taylor Pearson calls this The Turkey Problem, inspired by a clever analogy found in Nassim Taleb's *Black Swan*. Taleb writes:

> *"Consider a turkey that is fed every day. Every single feeding will firm up the bird's belief that it is the general rule of life to be fed every day by friendly members of the human race 'looking out for its best interests,' as a politician would say. On the afternoon of the Wednesday before Thanksgiving, something unexpected will happen to the turkey. It will incur a revision of belief."*

Bye-bye Mr. Turkey. The turkey thinks he's safe, until he realizes at the last minute that he's not. We tend to believe that working at big corporations keeps us safe. But in reality, it's the job of the HR department to make you feel that way, even if it's not true. Every day you work at a large corporation, you're building up silent risk. One day, you might realize you're a turkey. Do you remember a company called Lehman Brothers? I know it's a distant memory for some, but before 2008 it was the 4th largest investment bank in the United States. Then it went bankrupt. Bye-bye.

But bankruptcy isn't the only threat. A more likely outcome is that your job is stolen by a kind Indian man who speaks wonderful English and knows way more about your duties than you do. Or, maybe it's not a kind Indian man. Maybe it's a computer program, or a robot named iBob. You can see how the idea of a "safe career path" is starting to fade into the past.

If you subscribe to The Turkey Problem and subsequently decide to aim for something more entrepreneurial, there's certainly risk. But the risk is visible. And you have much tighter control over the outcome of any given situation. In this case, you're a cheetah. You're hunting for your own food. You're responsible for catching it. If you work hard and hunt, you eat. If you don't, you starve.

There's risk either way. So you have to ask yourself, do you want to be a turkey or a cheetah? Eventually you might have no choice. Turkeys could very well go extinct in your lifetime.

CONNECTIONS VS. CREATIONS: OR WHY YOUR PARENTS ARE LYING TO YOUR FACE

"It's not what you know, it's who you know." The expression is ubiquitous. We've all heard it. Our parents taught it to us a long time ago. We've read about it in 'How-To' books.

It's a nice narrative: Just befriend amazing people, and you can be amazing too! But how? How do we befriend them? The truth is that the *how* happens way before the connection is made.

A thousand years ago, if you were friends with the King, or a member of the aristocracy, your life was set. The main way to achieve this was to be born into the family (in other words, pure luck).

A hundred years ago, if you were friends with John D. Rockefeller, you had no worries. The best way to interact with him was to start an oil company of your own, and schedule some business meetings. Clearly, not an easy task. Heck, you had to strike oil!

Twenty-five years ago, if you were friends with a successful CEO, you were in good shape. In order to make that happen, you'd attend a university, get a job, and work your way up the corporate ladder until you were an exec. Then you'd befriend the CEO and the rest of the C-suite.

In all of these examples, if you know the most powerful people, you have a better chance at living a privileged life. If you don't know powerful people, you might still have an okay life, but you'll never experience an abundance of wealth. Note that it gets a little easier to know the guy at the top as we move forward in history. More importantly, the path to get there is less about luck, and more about hard work.

Because befriending the CEO (or reaching the C-suite) feels like a relatively attainable goal (compared to befriending a King, or a John D. Rockefeller), most us are fighting for that outcome these days. But about twenty-five years ago, something else happened that changed the entire game: The internet.

Being friends with a CEO is still valuable. The internet didn't make it unimportant to know powerful people. But it did change the rules of who gets to be powerful, and how that happens.

Before the internet, you had to get permission from the higher-ups to do anything substantial. You had to know the King. You had to work with institutions, like banks, to build a big business. Creating serious wealth (top 5% of earners) was a hobby reserved for the elite. It was for the incumbents. It only happened behind closed doors. If you wanted to join the party, you needed a gatekeeper to unlock the door and let you in.

Today, there aren't any doors. You don't need permission from anyone. You just need an internet connection and a computer.

Here's the new paradigm: It's no longer what you know, or who you know. It's what you create. This fundamental shift has been brought on by technologies (mainly the internet) that have made it insanely easy to create all kinds of awesome stuff. Want to become a published author? Go for it. You don't need a publisher. Just write your book and publish it on Amazon. I did this, and now I'm a bestselling author, selling more books than most authors would have dreamed of twenty years ago.

Want to sell a product? Go for it. You don't need a warehouse, or manufacturing equipment, or a storefront, or a bank to finance everything. Raise money on KickStarter, use Google to find a cheap manufacturer in China, and ship your product to customers all over the world on Amazon, or through your own ecommerce store. Want to learn how to start a company? You don't need to spend hundreds of thousands of dollars getting an MBA. Take a course on Udemy. Or, join a startup accelerator program—and they'll pay *you*.

Here's the thing. Even if you're not doing this stuff, other hustlers are. The trend is happening whether you like it or not. When new resources become readily available, a sliver of society inevitably flocks to those resources and uses them to their advantage, often reaping astronomically high rewards in the process.

The competitive advantage has shifted from connections to creations. Knowing important people is still important, but the means of meeting them has changed. The order is now reversed. You don't connect and then create. You create and then connect.

Getting a degree, getting hired, and working your way up the corporate ladder is no longer the quickest, safest, or smartest way to ascend into a position of power. In fact, it's a bad approach. Starting your own company (or building your own product) and becoming your own boss is a much better strategy. When you do impressive things on your own, other impressive people will want to connect with you.

Going to college used to be a bargaining chip. It's not anymore. This is the great misconception of our generation. It's the result of our parents telling us how things are supposed to work. The problem is that the system has changed dramatically over the past two decades.

A college degree is now a commodity. Everyone has one, so it carries no leverage. It won't help you befriend the CEO. The high-value skill in our economy has shifted to entrepreneurship—hustling. People who understand the fallacy of the 'who you know' argument stand to gain the most upward mobility and leverage in the era of technology. They will be the new Rockefellers. Your resources are limitless and free. The blank white screen is your laboratory. Go create stuff. It's no longer what you know or who you know. It's what you create.

BLINDERS

When you're hustling, you need to put blinders on. This is easier said than done. People will tell you your idea, or your project, or your dream won't work. That's fine. Let them worry. That's their job, not yours. You can't worry. You have to produce.

Here's what people will tell me when I show them this book: "This isn't original. This book isn't saying anything new. People don't really care about hustling. You need a better story. You need to do more research. You need endorsements. You need a big marketing budget and a launch strategy. You need an editor and a book designer." And my response will be: "Shhhh, I'm working."

CHAPTER 5

HUSTLER'S DIARY - DAY 2

Thursday, December 10th, 2015

12:40 p.m. It's past noon and I haven't started writing yet. You'd think "freakout mode" would be in full effect, but I actually feel fine. I wish I had started sooner, but I knew if I rushed into writing immediately, the content would be bad. I hope I made the right decision. What's done is done. Here's what's happened so far:

I woke up at 7 a.m., slightly sluggish but still hopeful for a productive day. I knew what I had in front of me—a long day full of writing. I chugged some water, scarfed down some vanilla yogurt, and ate an apple. Then I meditated for a bit, showered, and called a friend to clear my head. Next up was a big breakfast (two eggs, toast, mixed greens, grapes, tomato slices, and bacon). After that I worked out: Plyometrics—which is the hardest P90X workout for me. It's a lot of jumping and squatting, which makes me sweat. I downed some Emergen-c (energy drink) mixed with orange juice and five grams of creatine monohydrate during the workout, plus plenty of water.

Now I'm sitting here—ready to go…still sweating. I should probably rinse off again in the shower, but I'm feeling inspired and want to get straight to writing. Exercise does that for me. It's a trigger for good ideas. That's why it was worth it.

I need to write 10,000 words today. If I keep a pace of 1,000 words per hour, I'll hit 10,000 by around 11 p.m. It's a lot, but it's doable. If I did it yesterday, I can do it again. Sometimes, hustlers have to sprint. And this is a sprinting situation. If I can get to 30K words by tomorrow night, that gives me the weekend to proofread and edit.

I'm looking at my calendar right now. Monday is the 13th. I need the book in the Amazon store, (or purchasable on my own website) by the 20th so people have time to order it for Christmas. That's my goal, anyway.

1 p.m. I just spent five minutes researching Gum-Road, a payment provider that allows content creators to easily sell their work directly to consumers. I'm considering using this method. It might be easier than going through Amazon. I learned about Gumroad through doing research about self-publishing. I had it tucked away in the back of my head. There's a lesson here: Hustlers always need to be learning and self-teaching. You never know when dormant information will come in handy.

It's been another 30 minutes, and I've written about 500 words, even after researching Gum-road. I'm currently on track to log 10,000 words today. Nice! It's liberating, knowing that I have a single focus today. I don't have to worry about anything else. I've cleared my schedule. I've closed out of my email. The only tabs open on my computer screen are in relation to this project. The phone is on silent.

It's go time.

CHAPTER 6

HUSTLER HABITS AND TRICKS

Hustling requires more than just a shift in mindset. That mindset needs to actually inform your actions. The leap from mindset to taking action is a big one. But the actions themselves don't have to be big. You can start by making small adjustments, and slowly build up your skills.

Eventually, you'll notice yourself making decisions differently, prioritizing tasks differently, and spending your time differently. This chapter goes through the different habits and behaviors, large and small, that you should be cultivating as you wade deeper into hustling.

BREAK THE RULES

This book breaks a lot of rules. It's short. (Aren't books supposed to be long?) It's self-published. (Won't that make it less legit?) I'm not just the author. I'm the editor, the proofreader, the cover designer, the copywriter, the publisher, and the sales team. There's another book that initially used this method. It's called *50 Shades of Grey*. Maybe you've heard of it? The beauty of changing the rules is that it changes the game. When you change the game, you have an edge over your competitors. It's as if you're playing basketball, but you're allowed to run without dribbling, and your basket is twice the normal size. Your opponents are now confused and upset. No fair!

Here's the difference between basketball and life. There's no "referee of life." There's no one to call "foul!" if you break the rules a little bit. Yes, of course there are laws. Don't break those. But rules are different than laws. You can break the rules and get away with it.

When you realize breaking the rules is allowed in the game of life, your opportunities widen significantly. You'll be able to move more swiftly and overcome barriers you once thought were insurmountable. Why don't more people live this way? Fear. Fear of consequences, fear of ridicule, fear of being shamed. Guess what? Very few people actually care, and the few who do don't matter. They're likely just jealous.

Remember, I'm not talking about breaking laws. I'm not talking about hurting anyone or being malicious in any way. I'm talking about identifying trends and patterns that create the illusion of barriers, and then defying them. *College is the only path to success. Money leads to happiness. Writing a good resume is the best way to get hired.* Are these rules to live by? Or are they broad assumptions that create the illusion of a non-negotiable framework?

ASK "WHY?"

People love to follow. It's human nature. When we see a patterned behavior, we assume it's the right way to do things.

I was watching a show about social psychology on the science channel recently. They did an experiment. They invited a subject into a waiting room, under the guise that the subject would be interviewed for a study. Unbeknownst to the subject, the waiting room *was* the study.

Several other people were seated in chairs in the room. A few minutes after the test subject arrived, a bell rang. Everyone in the room, except the test subject, stood up for a moment, and then sat back down. A few minutes later, the process repeated. The test subject looked around nervously, wondering what this meant. Why was everyone standing up when the bell rang?

After a few more cycles, the test subject began standing up with everyone else. Why? Confusion and fear. Because everyone else was demonstrating a clear pattern of behavior, the test subject felt compelled to fall in line. This study was performed with multiple subjects, and nearly all of them joined the group and began standing up after a few cycles.

When you're hustling, you have to constantly fight the natural tendency to belong. Instead, question the world's assumptions. Learn to ask, "why?" Is money truly the only path to happiness? Or is that just something people say? Is college the only path to success? What if the strength of a college degree is weakening? What if there are other emerging options? And what is success, by the way? It's easy to follow the crowd. Questioning the mob is far more difficult. It's also where you'll find the biggest opportunities.

TAKE ADVANTAGE OF TRENDS

If you get good at identifying trends, you can use them to your advantage. Hustlers observe what the crowd is doing, and then ask, "How can I gain leverage from that behavior?"

One of the masters of trendspotting is Rohit Bhargava, author of *Non-Obvious*. He curates the biggest trends each year and packages them up into a book. Then he explains how people and businesses can take advantage of these trends to improve their position in the marketplace. Thinking deliberately about trends is a secret sauce for most successful hustlers, because it creates an unfair advantage.

When Evan Spiegel built Snapchat, he was capitalizing on a trend. He saw people using Facebook and their phones to share photos, but noticed they felt inhibited by the fact that the images were either permanent, or public. By reversing those two elements—making image-sharing ephemeral and private, he solved a big problem. Snapchat exploded across the younger demographics and quickly became a multibillion-dollar business.

Another example is Kik, a popular messaging app. When Kik launched, plenty of messaging services already existed. In fact, the ultimate messaging services seemed to be the ones already built into everyone's phones. Apple had a messaging app, and so did Android. So, why reinvent the wheel? Ted Livingston, the founder of Kik, had other ideas. Why? Because he had identified a trend.

Consumers were clearly upset with the built-in messaging services. First, the telecom companies were charging per message sent and received, which was a horrible experience. It felt like classic, capitalistic highway robbery. Second—and this was a big problem for teens: You could only exchange messages by giving out your phone number.

Livingston noticed that teens wanted to chat with other people they met online, but had no safe way of doing that without giving out their number. So he created Kik, which allows people to create a username instead. Kiksters can then share their username to start chatting, while keeping their digits private. But even better, messaging is unlimited, and completely free.

By examining the trends happening in the messaging market, Livingston was able to build a product that rivaled the multi-billion dollar incumbents. Now *his* company is valued at over a billion.

WORK SMARTER **AND** HARDER

Hustling isn't just about working smarter, or harder. It's both. The best hustlers find shortcuts, but then accelerate through them. They have an engine that rarely turns off. There's a delicate balance to this. Efficiency does not equal effectiveness. If you're efficiently working on something that's not effective, you're not being productive. Read that last sentence a few more times.

You need to be working both efficiently and effectively. More hours doesn't equal more productivity. Frequent breaks and rejuvenating activities have been shown to increase productivity over the long haul. That said, you need to cultivate a puritan work ethic and keep the motor running more often than not. There is no single shortcut to success, only small efficiencies along the way.

SELF-TEACH

> *"Everybody who has a smartphone, which is pretty soon going to be everybody in the world, has the Library of Congress in their pocket. So that means a girl growing up in Bangladesh now, has a better library than a student at Columbia or Harvard had twenty years ago."* —Ben Horowitz

Learning has become abundantly accessible. The internet has changed the game. There's plenty of crap on the internet—don't get me wrong. But there's good stuff, too.

One of the strongest pieces of advice I can give you is to read more. I don't care how much you're reading. Do it more. Reading is the great equalizer. It turns hopeful dreamers into doers. It turns amateurs into experts. It opens our minds to new perspectives and thought patterns. It breeds confidence. Once you start reading, you'll be inclined to teach yourself other things. Music, art, software development, cooking, math. It's the ultimate gateway drug to expanding your horizons, and your skills.

You no longer need to wait for the gatekeepers to choose you. Don't wait for that university to tell you you're smart enough. Don't wait for that company to separate your resume from the pile. Get out there and learn on your own. Create on your own. Grow on your own. Before you know it, the universities and corporations will be begging you to join them. And then *you'll* be in the position of power—to say yes, or no.

Quick Tips:

For paid courses on pretty much everything, look into Udemy and Team Treehouse, which are both listed in the bonus material. For gaining knowledge through reading, start with the books listed in the bonus material as well. You can then find similar content by browsing the Kindle store's recommendations, which are based on your purchase history. You don't need a Kindle to read digital books. Kindle books can be viewed on any phone, tablet, or computer. More reading and learning tips in the following section...

GATHER INSPIRATION

Where do hustlers find ideas and motivation to get over the hump, or get an edge? These are the tools and tricks I use:

1. **Feedly** - Feedly is my feed reader. I subscribe to 30-40 blogs. Most of them are tech blogs, or

the personal blogs of thought leaders I admire. I'll name a few: TechCrunch, VentureBeat, GigaOm, Feld Thoughts (Brad Feld), AVC (Fred Wilson), Zen Habits (Leo Babauta), FourHourWorkweek (Tim Ferriss), TheMinimalists. Blogs are an amazing source of inspiration.

2. **Podcasts** - I love listening to podcasts because you can do it hands free. Going for a run? Stuck in traffic? At the gym? Listen to a podcast. My favorite right now is *The Tim Ferriss Show*. There are a handful of stories in this book pulled from his episodes, including the story of how Jamie Foxx got his name. You'll find gems of inspiration if you just put your headphones on and listen. Another good one is *Entrepreneur on Fire* with John Lee Dumas.

3. **Amazon** - This is a hack. As you know, Amazon sells books. Lots of books. Books are arguably the best place to find information. The problem is they cost money. I don't know about you, but I don't have the money to buy every book on my wish list. Luckily, there's a trick that gives you access to some of the best content for free: Read the samples! Amazon has a feature called "Look Inside" that allows you to read a sample of a book. They sometimes show quite

a bit of content, upwards of 10-20% of the entire book. Books are usually written such that the best content comes first. The author wants to hook you in. Also, the beginning of books often contain a summary (i.e. this book will cover x, y, and z). By reading the samples, you can get a good sense for what the book is about, find good quotes, and absorb the main principles that are likely to push your mind forward. I use this method constantly. If you look at the quotes I've used from other books, and then search those books on Amazon, you'll often find that the quote comes early in the text. There's a good chance I never bought the book. I just read the sample.

4. **Medium** - Medium is, by far, my favorite blogging platform. It was founded by Ev Williams, one of the founders of Twitter. Ev knows how to build beautiful products, particularly communication platforms. Before Medium and Twitter, he built Blogger, another blogging platform. This is what he does. It's his passion. And he delivers. Medium is possibly the easiest way to both share and consume content. The interface is exquisite, both from a reading and writing perspective, and their software does a tremendous job of feeding you high-quality content

that you'll find interesting. Based on who you follow and your interests, you'll receive a daily email digest with recommended articles to read. Their emails never feel spammy to me. They always feel useful and engaging. I use Medium both as a way to send my ideas out into the world, and as a way to gather the ideas of others.

5. **Product Hunt** - Product Hunt is exactly what it sounds like. It's a platform for sharing and finding amazing products. PH started primarily with tech products, but they've expanded to include pretty much anything. They now have subcategories for tech, games, podcasts, and books. I expect more categories will be added in the future. PH also has a feature called "Collections," which are groupings of products or ideas. Browsing the site can turn up some amazing resources.

USE PROCESS HACKS

There's an endless list of techniques for boosting productivity, but here are a few quick-wins everyone should employ:

The Power of Habit

Use your calendar, or the reminder app on your phone, to give yourself cues to stay on track. I have daily reminders to:

- Eat breakfast
- Eat lunch
- Eat dinner
- Get ready for bed

Even though these are obvious, it helps to have a reminder. Sometimes I don't follow them exactly when they pop-up, but it still guards against waiting too long, or forgetting completely.

The Power of Constraints

Set constraints for yourself. I started doing P90X several years ago and gained forty pounds of muscle in ninety days. I got incredible results because P90X has built-in constraints. The program is set up to be ninety days for a reason.

This book is an exercise in setting constraints, too. Writing a book in three days sounds crazy, but by specifying a ridiculously short timetable, I've been working my ass off to get it done. And I just might hit my mark.

The Power of a Minimalist Working Space

Your working space should include only four things:

1. A surface
2. A computer
3. A chair (unless you have a standing desk)
4. Water (preferably in a glass or bottle)

These are the only things you need in order to be productive. If you enjoy listening to music while you work, you can add headphones to the list. The fewer things you have in your working space, the better your work will be. To take this a step further, remove icons from your desktop screen. (You can still keep programs and files on your desktop, while hiding the icons. Do a google search to figure out how to do that.) While you're working, close any tabs that aren't relevant. Track your time with tools like Toggl or RescueTime.

FOCUS

> *"The way to get the most out of your work and your life is to go as small as possible."*
>
> —Gary Keller, The One Thing

Gary Keller knows the power of focus. He's written an entire book about it. *The One Thing* reached #1 on the Wallstreet Journal bestseller list in 2013. The book is aptly titled. The entire premise revolves around finding one thing to focus on. Gary argues that if you cultivate this laser focus, you'll make the right decisions over and over again. And over time, all those decisions will add up to huge success. So ask yourself, what's the one thing you can do this week such that by doing it, everything else would be easier or unnecessary?

Beyond decision-making, you need to find the one thing you want to be good at. Apple is known for its unparalleled design. Google is known for its unparalleled search performance. BMW's slogan is "We only do one thing" (cars).

Don't freak out. You don't have to only do one thing for the rest of your life. You just have to do one thing right now. That's how you get really good. In other words, do one thing at a time. Pro athletes often become broadcasters after they're done playing on the field. Some of them also end up going into business. Do they do all of those things at the same time? No. They do them separately. If you spread yourself too thin, you can't become truly great at any one thing. If you're broadcasting the game, you can't also be the star on the field. You have to focus and choose one or the other.

PROTECT YOUR TEMPLE

You temple is your body. It's how you navigate the world. You have to treat it as a sacred part of your success plan. Hustlers often forget this and eventually run out of gas—which is a massive setback. Sometimes it's the nail in the coffin. When you're running on empty, you crash. And when you crash, you lose all momentum.

As we've already covered, it's really hard to get momentum back after it's lost. To avoid hitting the wall, you have to regularly care for your temple. There are obvious ways to do this, but it's worth reading through them. You need to internalize these habits and work them into your daily practice.

Relax

First, you need to relax. You need to slow down. If you find yourself in the Zone, you might be able to run on sheer adrenaline for awhile, but eventually you need to catch your breath. Realize that you're on this planet to enjoy yourself, not to win.

The Pomodoro Technique is a popular method for achieving extreme productivity. Interestingly, relaxing is part of the formula. The general concept is to have extreme focus for twenty-five minutes, followed by a break of five minutes. This process repeats itself, creating periods of "catching your breath" and decompression throughout your day.

I haven't officially used the Pomodoro Technique, but I follow a similar working pattern. The point is that *breaks help*. Start working them into your schedule. Welcome them as a time to appreciate your effort and recenter your body and mind. Here are some good things to do during breaks:

- Smile
- Breathe deeply
- Close your eyes
- Stretch your arms over your head and down to your toes
- Walk around
- Drink water
- Go to the bathroom
- Splash water on your face
- Do a few push-ups
- Listen to soothing music

Below are some things you should *not* do on your breaks. Instead, integrate them into your work

time, or include them in your downtime after finishing work for the day. *Dont*:

- Look at your to-do list
- Look at email
- Think about what you have to do next
- Open a bunch of tabs on your computer
- View social networking sites

Sleep

Sleep is grossly underappreciated. You might think,
as a hustler, you should learn to sleep less. This
couldn't be further from the truth. Remember the
difference between efficiency and effectiveness?
Sleeping four hours a night isn't helpful if that
means only two of your twenty waking hours are
productive. It makes far more sense to sleep for
eight hours, log 5-10 hours of ultra productive
work, and then relax for the remainder. People tend
to forget that sleep is fuel. You can't run without it.
The same goes for nourishment.

Eat

Eating well has become a lost art. We take two
minutes to heat something up in the microwave, or
shovel fastfood into our mouths, or eat processed
junk from the store. Start etching out more time in

your schedule to actually cook and eat well. Again, this will improve your efficiency and effectiveness over the long run. Here are some quick tips:

- *Eat more greens.* Try adding greens to every meal. I like asparagus or arugula. Asparagus and eggs for breakfast is fantastic.
- *Eat real food.* Meaning unprocessed meats, fruits, vegetables, and grains.
- *Eat snacks.* Snacks keep your metabolism going and guard against energy crashes. Don't snack on donuts. Snack on just nuts. See what I did there?
- *Avoid coffee.* Coffee gets you high, but then causes you to crash. For sustained energy, cut it out of your diet. A good replacement is fruit, which contains complex carbs. The slow burning sugars in fruit will give you an energy boost when you first eat it, but also sustained energy throughout the day. I like small, red apples. Crisp, sweet, and a good size for a quick snack. If you need something to replace your routine of drinking a hot beverage, try tea instead.

Drink Water

Most of us don't get enough water. Do you ever feel yourself getting grumpy as you work? Do you get headaches in the afternoons? Chances are you're dehydrated and just need some water. When your body is starved for water, standard operations become difficult. Thinking becomes blurred, patience fades into intolerance, etc.

Thankfully, there's a simple solution: Carry a water bottle with you wherever you go. I use the Nalgene Tritan Wide Mouth BPA Free Water Bottle - 1 Quart Size. This tiny purchase has saved me from insanity on multiple occasions. If you keep your water bottle nearby, you'll find that drinking becomes habit. Once you're effortlessly getting enough water without thinking about it, you'll consistently perform at a higher level.

Meditate

Meditating sounds bourgy, but it's not. Everyone should do it. Meditating doesn't have to include "ohms", or sitting cross-legged on the floor, or breathing weird. Meditating is simply about relaxing your mind and letting your thoughts rest. Here's how I meditate:

1. Set a timer for 10-20 minutes, depending on my mood.
2. Sit up against my bedrest, against a wall, or cross-legged on the floor (this just happens to be my preference).
3. Close my eyes.
4. Relax my mind as much as possible until the timer goes off.

Sometimes I'll count my breaths and try to breathe slowly. Sometimes I'll move my arms and head around, basically stretching. Whenever I catch myself thinking (about anything), I'll bring my focus back to the space between my eyes. Then I'll try to "look" at that spot, with my eyes still closed.

The act of coming back to nothingness evokes a sense of peace, and that's what makes meditation so powerful. If you can feel that moment of nothingness for even twenty seconds out of a twenty-minute session, that's a successful session. You'll open your eyes feeling refreshed, relaxed, and rejuvenated. Like you just took a power nap.

Exercise

In *The Four Hour Body*, Tim Ferriss writes about an exclusive event hosted by Sir Richard Branson on his private island. Someone asked Branson for his best advice on being productive. He paused for a moment, and then calmly answered: "Work out." Exercise is typically seen as a daunting task. Why?

Two reasons:

1. There's not enough time.
2. It's hard.

I'll dispel #1 first. You can get meaningful results from exercising in twenty minutes or less. If you can't find twenty minutes, you need to figure out how to regain control of your life. Beyond that, exercising actually increases your productivity later in the day when you're working. Which of these two scenarios makes better use of eight hours? (Hint: It's #2):

1. Four hours of grogginess mixed with 4 hours of productive work
2. One hour of breaks and eating +0.33 hours of exercise + 6.67 hours of productive work

Here's a routine you can do in twenty minutes to make your entire day more productive:

1. 0:30 Jog in place

2. 0:30 Jumping Jacks
3. 0:30 Roll head from side to side
4. 0:30 With legs spread wide, bend over and rock back and forth
5. 0:30 Push-ups
6. 0:30 Pull-ups
7. 0:30 Rest
8. 0:30 Push-ups
9. 0:30 Pull-ups
10. 0:30 Rest
11. 0:30 Push-ups
12. 0:30 Pull-ups
13. 0:30 Rest
14. 0:30 Sit-ups
15. 0:30 Hold Plank Position
16. 0:30 Rest
17. 0:30 Sit-ups
18. 0:30 Hold Plank Position
19. 1:00 Rest
20. Repeat 1-19

Notice I didn't include repetition counts. That's deliberate. Do as many as you can in the time allotted. Keep track of your numbers during each session and strive to increase them over time. For pull-ups, you can get a hanging doorway bar for under $30.

No complicated installation required. It will fit into most doorways without a problem.[4]

Now on to #2, "It's hard." Guess what? Life is hard. Suck it up. With consistency comes progress. After a month of working out consistently, you won't dread it anymore. In fact, you might start looking forward to it.

---

[4] There's a link to my favorite pull-up bar in the bonus material section.

CHAPTER 7

HUSTLER'S DIARY - DAY 3

Friday, December 11th, 2015

8 a.m. I've been up for about 30 minutes. I went to bed at 11:30 last night and woke at 7:30. Guess I was tired! I purposefully didn't use an alarm. That might sound crazy given the fact that I'm supposed to finish my book today, but I knew I wouldn't perform well if I didn't sleep. I only logged 8,500 words yesterday. It will be difficult to reach 30,000 by the end of today, but that's okay. I'm making amazing progress. When you're hustling, you have to realize you won't always hit your goals exactly as you initially set them. Goals are meant to push you, and I'm certainly pushing myself. That's good enough.

I went through my typical routine immediately after waking up: Drink water, pee, wash face, brush teeth. Then I downed some yogurt. What next? Breakfast? Write? Nope. Dishes. You might be thinking, "Why worry about the dishes right now? You're supposed to be sprinting to the finish line! You don't have time for that!" You're wrong, for two reasons:

1. *A clean home is a clean mind. I can't work when there's clutter. This sounds silly, but try it for yourself. It makes a huge difference. Remember, the optimal working space is one that's practically empty.*

2. *Doing the dishes is a passive exercise, which means your mind is free to wander. I was extremely worried about hitting my content goals when I woke up this morning. I wasn't sure what to write about. How would I ever get to 30,000 words? But once I started washing dishes, the ideas came flooding in. Now I'm sitting here, in my clean apartment, ready to write.*

Yesterday I decided to eat a huge breakfast and workout before writing. Today, I'm pushing those things off until later. I want to make sure I put a dent in my work, to avoid feeling pressured in the afternoon and evening. That's a tip for all you hustlers: Build routines, not schedules. Routines are more like habits. I have morning habits, and workout habits, and eating habits. A schedule, by contrast, is a sequential list of operations that make up your day. (Wake up, then workout, then eat, then go to a meeting, etc.)

The problem with schedules is that they're too rigid. They don't allow for flexibility or creativity. When you're hustling and you're creating something, you need to be flexible. Our minds aren't always primed to be productive at exactly the same time every day. If you practice positive routines that become habit, but allow your schedule to be flexible, you'll optimize your performance.

I don't workout at the same time every day. I do it when it works best for me. If someone wants to meet with me to discuss a partnership or opportunity, I'm able to work it into my schedule because I know I can move other things around. I also don't go to bed at the same time every day. Instead, I go to bed when I'm ready to sleep, and wake up when I'm ready to wake up. If I need to set an alarm, I won't set it for a time (i.e. 6 a.m.). Instead, I'll set my timer to countdown from either 6.5 or 8 hours. I use those time intervals because

R.E.M sleep happens in 90 minute cycles. To avoid feeling groggy, it's best to wake up after a full cycle ends. So the intervals, in hours, are: 1.5, 3, 4.5, 6, 7.5, 9, etc. I set my timer for 6.5 or 8 because I've found I need about 30 minutes to settle down before I actually get into a sleep cycle.

When it comes to routines and schedules, experiment and see what works best for you. You might find that unless you workout at the exact same time every day, you'll skip workouts. If that's the case, you may need to be more rigid with yourself for that particular task. The only rule of the hustler is: There are no rules. You have to figure out your own way. So take everything I say with a grain of salt. Consider my advice, then construct your ideal system.

Back to the dishes. While I was scrubbing my plates, I started asking myself where I could find content to inspire my writing. I thought I'd share my list, which can now be found in the bonus material at the back of the book. By the way, with this diary entry I'm already at 700 words.

This is exactly the jumpstart I needed.

CHAPTER 8

HUSTLER TRAITS

What the hell are you doing?

I'm hanging. Helps me think.

hustle

Hustlers do all kinds of crazy things. That's because they're not afraid of experimentation, failing, being laughed at, or making a mistake. They know exploration leads to growth. This section examines the basic traits most hustlers have in common.

THEY'RE REALLY WEIRD

Everyone has strange ticks and habits. Embrace them. Habits help us stay grounded. Here are some unconventional habits from a few hustlers you may have heard about. These excerpts are all from the book *Daily Rituals*, by Mason Currey.

Ludwig van Beethoven
"His breakfast was coffee, which he prepared himself with great care—he determined that there should be sixty beans per cup, and he often counted them out one by one for a precise dose."

"Beethoven's unusual bathing habits are worth noting here. His pupil and secretary Anton Schindler recalled them in the biography, *Beethoven As I Knew Him*:

Washing and bathing were among the most pressing necessities of Beethoven's life. In this respect he was indeed an Oriental: to his way of thinking, Mohammed did not exaggerate a whit in the number of ablutions he prescribed. If he did not dress to go out during the morning working hours, he would stand in great déshabillé at his washstand and pour large pitchers of water over his hands, bellowing up and down the scale or sometimes humming loudly to himself. Then he would stride around his room with rolling or staring eyes, jot something down, then resume his pouring of water and loud singing. These were moments of deep meditation, to which no one could have objected but for two unfortunate circumstances. First of all, the servants would often burst out laughing. This made the master angry and he would sometimes assault them in language that made him cut an even more ridiculous figure. Or, secondly, he would come into conflict with the landlord, for all too often, so much water was spilled that it went right through the floor."

Benjamin Franklin

"At the time, baths in cold water were considered a tonic, but Franklin believed the cold was too much of a shock to the system. He wrote in a letter:

I have found it much more agreeable to my consti-tution to bathe in another element, I mean cold air. With this view I rise early almost every morning, and sit in my chamber without any clothes what-ever, half an hour or an hour, according to the season, either reading or writing. This practice is not in the least painful, but on the contrary, agree-able, and if I return to bed afterwards, before I

dress myself, as sometimes happens, I make a sup-
plement to my night's rest, of one or two hours of
the most pleasing sleep that can be imagined."

Pablo Picasso

"The Montparnasse apartment was not without its bohemianism, however. Picasso took over its large, airy studio, forbade anyone from entering without his permission, and surrounded himself with his painting supplies, piles of miscellaneous junk, and a menagerie of pets, including a dog, three Siamese cats, and a monkey named Monina."[5]

One of my weird habits is excessive showering. Sometimes I shower four times in a single day. I'll often take one in the morning, one before working out, one after working out, and one at night. Showers help me relax, give me new ideas, and refresh my body and mind. The recommendation to shower more often came from my father. Whenever I told him I felt stuck, he'd ask, "Did you shower yet?"

---

[5] Note that Picasso's setup doesn't follow my advice of having a minimalist working space. Just a reminder that everyone's different, and you need to create your own ideal reality.

THEY'RE CREATIVE

A few days before I decided to write this book, the concept was already brewing in my head, without me knowing it. On a whim, I released a post on Medium, my favorite blogging platform. I didn't re-release it on my website because it was super short. It was a post about making moves—making something happen. I've copied it here:

Stop talking about creating something awesome. Instead, go and do it. Release it to the world. Didn't go viral? Try again. You'll get better. There is no silver bullet. Fear, inaction, and failing to try one more time are your biggest obstacles.

Stop jotting down good ideas.

Stop thinking.

Stop reading this.

Start doing.

Take action. Create. Create. Create. Repeat.

Virality shouldn't even be your goal. Think of it instead as a well-deserved reward for producing something worthwhile. Producing something worthwhile is your goal. And to do that, the very first step—the mandatory first step, is to produce.

The post actually went viral, to a degree. A few days after its release, it was already one of my most popular articles. There are a few lessons here:

1. Content doesn't have to be long to be good.
2. Content doesn't have to be deep to be good. Clever also works.
3. There are different strategies for creating content. This obviously wasn't meant to be an epic post. I wrote it in five minutes. It was done primarily as an experiment to gauge whether or not people would find that type of content share-worthy. The answer was yes.

Being Creative and Off-the-Cuff Can Lead to Crazy Results

One of Tim Ferriss' most popular videos on YouTube is a video titled "How to Peel a Hard Boiled Egg Without Peeling." It's a one minute video filmed on a crappy camera (maybe a phone).

Tim has said he had no idea it would be so popular. Over the course of his career, Tim has spent tens of thousands of dollars creating professionally produced marketing videos for his books and other products, yet a simple, amateur video about peeling a hard boiled egg resulted in the highest view count. Getting creative like this can generate mind-blowing results. Here's another example from my own life:

When my first startup was in its infancy, we didn't really know what we were going to build. The Facebook platform opened shortly after we formed the company, so we created an app called StickyNotes. The app was very simple, but it worked. It was a way to send personalized messages back and forth between friends. As the app grew, so did our opportunities. But we didn't see long-term value in StickyNotes. We saw it as a way to bridge the gap until we were able to create bigger and better things.

At one point, we were strapped for cash. If we didn't make some money quickly, we'd go out of business. So, we stopped everything we were doing and began working on a few banner ad campaigns that we could release on StickyNotes. Since we had plenty of users, we figured it could generate some money and help us live to see another day. It was around Valentine's Day, and we had been working with an ad partner who told us they had campaigns for various chatting applications that performed well during the holiday.

We quickly whipped up the ads and integrated them into Sticky Notes. The next day, on Valentine's Day, we made $75,000. It was enough to keep us going for at least another 1-2 months.

Getting creative means finding the single most important thing to be working on to keep you going in the right direction, even if that means working on something besides your number one goal. If you can't pay the bills, the big idea doesn't matter.

THEY MAKE IT WORK

Naval Ravikant has figured out how to read more. The solution is to read less. Yes, it sounds nonsensical. I love when that happens. Let me explain.

Here's the scenario: You've decided you're going to become an avid reader. You'll read at least one book a week. You just need to cultivate the habit of reading, and then it'll become second nature. This is how habits are formed, right? It's totally going to work.

So, you start adding books to your Kindle library. *"Oh, this one is supposed to be good. Yes! Lots of reviews on this other one. Add it to the list!"* Before you know it, you've got fifty great books lined up. You're pumped. You should be able to get through these in a year, or maybe even faster!

Then reality sets in. It's week one, and you're halfway through your first book. But you've hit a slump. The beginning was good, but it got a little boring in the middle. Week two rolls around. You're still stuck in the middle of book one. Crap. This isn't going to work. Fail.

Enter Naval Ravikant. Naval is the CEO of AngelList, but he's also a prolific reader. He reads ten to twenty books at a time, and he's read thousands over the course of his life. How does Naval do it? Simple. When he gets bored (as we all do), he just stops reading and moves to the next book. He doesn't place any value on finishing, or reading books from cover to cover. He just reads as much, or as little, as he wants. He treats books like throwaway blog posts or tweets. If you take this approach, the "I'm stuck" problem goes away.

Here are Naval's thoughts on the topic, in his own words (transcribed from a podcast with Tim Ferriss):

"We're taught from a young age that books are something you finish. Books are sacred. When you go to school and you're assigned to read a book, you have to finish the book. So...we get this contradiction where everyone I know is stuck on some book. So what do you do? You give up on reading books for a while.

That, for me, was a tragedy because I grew up on books, and then I switched to blogs, and then I switched to Twitter and Facebook. And then I realized I wasn't actually learning anything. I was just taking little dopamine snacks all day long.

[So] I came up with this hack where I started treating books as throwaway blog posts or as bite-sized Tweets or Facebook posts, and I felt no obligation to finish any book. So now, anytime someone mentions a book to me, a buy it. At any given time, I'm reading somewhere between ten and twenty books. I'm flipping through them. So if the book is getting a little boring, I'll skip ahead. Sometimes I'll start reading a book in the middle because some paragraph caught my eye, and I'll just continue from there. And I feel no obligation whatsoever to finish the book. If at some point I decide the book is boring, or if it's got pieces of it

that are incorrect—so now I can't trust the rest of the information in there, I just delete it. And I don't remember them at all.

So I treat books now as other people might treat throwaway, light pieces of information on the web. And all of the sudden, books are back into my reading library. And that's great, because there's a lot of ancient wisdom in there."

Absolutely brilliant. After listening to Naval, I realized I was already using his hack inadvertently. But I was doing it poorly. I would get stuck, stop reading, and then move on to another book. But then I would keep going back to the original book in hopes of finishing it. Now I just delete the books I'm stuck on, or skip passed the parts I don't find interesting. It's not that a book is useless if it can't be read from cover to cover. The reality is that most books have really amazing sections, but aren't mind-blowing all the way through.

Reading is suddenly approachable again. Thank you, Naval.

THEY'RE DEAF TO DOUBTERS

My grandmother forwards me clever emails all the time. Sometimes I just hit "delete." But sometimes I save them. Recently, she sent me a good one about naysayers. It reminded me that opinions, even from respected leaders, are often wrong. Here are some of the more entertaining excerpts from the email:

"We don't like their sound, and guitar music is on the way out." —Decca Recording Company on declining to sign the Beatles in 1962

"This 'telephone' has too many shortcomings to be seriously considered as a means of communication. The device is inherently of no value to us." —Western Union internal memo, 1876

"Rail travel at high speed is not possible because passengers, unable to breathe, would die of asphyxia." —Dr. Dionysius Lardner, 1830

"I think there is a world market for maybe five computers." —Thomas Watson, chairman of IBM, 1943.

"Everyone acquainted with the subject will recognize it as a conspicuous failure." —Henry Morton, president of the Stevens Institute of Technology, on Edison's light bulb, 1880.

"The horse is here to stay but the automobile is only a novelty—a fad." —The president of the Michigan Savings Bank advising Henry Ford's lawyer not to invest in the Ford Motor Company, 1903.

"Television won't last because people will soon get tired of staring at a plywood box every night." —Darryl Zanuck, movie producer, 20th Century Fox, 1946.

"There is no reason for any individual to have a computer in his home." —Ken Olson, president, chairman, and founder of Digital Equipment Corporation, 1977.

"There will never be a bigger plane built." —A Boeing engineer, after the first flight of the 247, a twin engine plane that holds ten people.

"How sir, would you make a ship sail against the wind and currents by lighting a bonfire under the deck? I pray you, excuse me, I have not the time to listen to such nonsense." —Napoleon Bonaparte, when told of Robert Fulton's steamboat, 1800's.

"The world potential market for copying machines is 5,000 at most" —IBM, to the eventual founders of Xerox, saying the photocopier had no market large enough to justify production, 1959.

"It'll be gone by June." —Variety Magazine on Rock n' Roll, 1955.

"A rocket will never be able to leave the earth's atmosphere." —The New York Times, 1936

There will always be naysayers. They'll heckle you, laugh at you, and ridicule you. Pay no attention to them. People will say this book is crap. They'll say it has no value. They'll give me a one star review. They'll say it's dumb because I wrote it in three days. I'm okay with that. As long as some people get value out of it, I'm happy to ignore the naysayers.

Peter Thiel's Hustler Barometer

Peter Thiel is a prolific investor. He was one of the first investors in Facebook. In most initial meetings with prospective portfolio companies, he asks, "What important truth do very few people agree with you on?" Thiel does this because it separates the true entrepreneurs from the fakes. If an entrepreneur has conviction about their idea, they'll stand by it, even in the face of doubt from others. Further, if the idea is doubted by most, it's a big idea. If it's accepted by most, it's too common to be valuable.

Boldly Go Where No (Hu)Man Has Gone Before

John Lee Dumas is the founder and creator of Entrepreneur on Fire, a popular podcast that reaches over a million listeners per month. He has been featured in *Forbes, Fast Company, Inc. Magazine, MSNBC,* and *Success Magazine.*

JLD had a crazy idea when he started EOFire. He thought, "What if I launch a 7-day podcast?" (meaning a new episode every day). This was unheard of at the time, and it's still rare today. John's mentors said it would never work. But he disagreed. He launched his 7-Day podcast and blew everyone's expectations out of the water. He's now a known celebrity in the podcasting world, making millions of dollars per year.

But here's the craziest part of the story: JLD only records interviews once per week! He stacks them up, doing seven interviews in a row. Then he has the rest of the week to relax, or enhance his business further with other efforts. That's called working smarter. John ignored the naysayers, hustled, and turned his dream into a reality.

THEY PREFER DOING OVER PLANNING

> *"Things may come to those who wait, but only the things left by those who hustle"*
>
> —*Abraham Lincoln*

Business schools used to teach entire classes on writing business plans. I'm sure some still do. Business plans, if you aren't familiar, are exactly what they sound like—future plans for a business. They're projections that forecast a company's expenses, revenues, and profitability over time. They also include things like marketing strategies and growth plans.

Business plans are bullshit. Any investor using a business plan as a gauge for anything other than writing skills is fooling themselves. It's impossible to accurately forecast a company's future metrics, especially in an early stage company that has yet to establish a sustainable business model. The business world is changing constantly, at an increasing rate. New technologies are being built, entire industries are rising and falling, society's behavioral patterns are evolving and subsequently affecting the relevance of existing products and services. How can a business accurately forecast what it will be doing five years from now, considering all of these constantly changing variables? It can't.

So what's the purpose of a business plan? The business plan makes people feel better—that's it. It's a BS report that says, (with zero data, mind you), "Everything in the future will be glorious! There's nothing to worry about!"

If you speak to savvy investors, they'll tell you to stop presenting your business plan, and ask you to start presenting your product. They prefer this because they know the business plan will change. And while the product will change too, it's a much better indicator of the company's current capabilities and future potential. The product is tangible. It's real.

The business plan, like many things in the business world, maps perfectly to the social world. Many of us get caught up in creating our life plan. Like a business plan, the life plan is the forecast of our life. "In five years I will be married. I will have $100,000 in the bank and a two year old child." This is an abridged version of a life plan. Most people take it way further than that. The life plan, just like the business plan, is a hoax. There is no way to accurately predict what life will throw at you, or what you'll be doing ten, five, or even one year from now.

When you create a life plan, you set yourself up for disappointment and frustration. Your life will undoubtedly take unforeseen twists and turns that will send you off course. When you lose your job, it'll feel like a setback. When you're behind schedule in finding the partner of your dreams, your relationships will become strained and forced. When unexpected expenses cut into your savings, you'll become anxious that your actual account balance doesn't match with whatever you had originally forecasted.

When you create a life plan, you narrow your scope of reality and become blind to opportunities that exist outside of that reality. This will drive you to make ill-advised decisions. Should you get married based on the current calendar year? Of course not. Should you continue learning about x, when the market is changing rapidly and rendering that knowledge obsolete? No! Smack yourself.

Everything around us is constantly changing. Being able to adapt is critical. Creating a rigid plan works against you because it prevents you from factoring in our changing environment. Stop planning and pretending you've got everything figured out. You don't.

Hustlers don't get caught up in the planning stage. Their primary instincts are to act, assess, and react.

THEY REJECT AUTHORITY

Comedian Louis C.K. was fed up with the big distributors who were putting his shows on DVD and making them available on iTunes. Sometimes they wouldn't send him royalty checks, and he had zero control over the pricing. So he decided to reject them. After self-producing one of his shows at the Beacon Theater in New York City, he put the recording online and sold it directly to his fans for $5. The result? He made over a million bucks in ten days.

In true rebel fashion, he then set aside $250,000 to cover the costs of the show, handed out another $250,000 to his staff as bonuses, and donated $280,000 to charities. "I never viewed money as being 'my money,'" he said. "I always saw it as 'The money.' It's a resource. If it pools up around me, then it needs to be flushed back out into the system. If I make another million, I'll give more of it away." Who needs institutional authorities when you can hustle instead?

THEY THINK DIFFERENT

"Be daring and choose to be different, even if it's unpopular. Thinking uniquely will lead to exceptional outcomes, while doing things as others do will result in more of the same. Defy the norm, be curious, and don't accept the status quo."

—Jonathan Alpert, author of Be Fearless: Change Your Life in 28 Days

Think Different was a slogan used by Apple in 1997.[6] Part of the campaign included a commercial known as The Crazy Ones. The narration goes like this:

Here's to the crazy ones. The misfits. The rebels. The troublemakers. The round pegs in the square holes. The ones who see things differently. They're not fond of rules. And they have no respect for the status quo. You can quote them, disagree with them, glorify or vilify them. About the only thing you can't do is ignore them. Because they change

---

[6] https://en.wikipedia.org/wiki/Think_different

things. They push the human race forward. And while some may see them as the crazy ones, we see genius. Because the people who are crazy enough to think they can change the world, are the ones who do.

It's easy to dismiss this campaign as grandiose, hyperbolic, and idealistic. But it's not. Big changes are usually the result of a bunch of little changes strung together. That's how big changes happen.

Thinking differently doesn't guarantee we'll change the world, but it gives us a better chance. And any change we bring about could potentially sow the seeds of a bigger change in the future. Don't trivialize your impact. Most of us don't think beyond what we know, or what's expected of us. It's hard to think different. But if we train ourselves to do it, it starts to come naturally.

THEY DO THE UNTHINKABLE

Casey Neistat isn't known for being traditional. At 34, he still looks like a rockstar. He's an accomplished YouTube creator, and he tends to think outside the box when it comes to media. In 2011, he produced a video called "Bike Lanes." In the video, Casey makes fun of the New York City Police Department's policies on ticketing bikers who ride outside the bike lanes. The video shows Casey running into all kinds of objects obstructing the designated bike lane—including a police cruiser. Time Magazine ranked Bike Lanes at #8 on their list of Top 10 Creative Videos of 2011. But Casey was just getting started.

In 2012, he produced a promotional video for Nike called Make It Count. Instead of following Nike's plan for the video, though, he decided to travel around the world using the budget Nike had given him. Despite deliberately rejecting Nike's agenda, the video went viral and amassed over three million views within the first five days of airing. Nike, as the story goes, was both surprised and pleased by the results.

THEY THINK BIG

Elon Musk thinks big. Previously a cofounder of PayPal, he now runs both Tesla (a company that builds electric cars) and SpaceX (a company that builds rocket ships). He's also the brains behind some intense side projects, like the *HyperLoop*, a super fast transit system that might one day take passengers from San Francisco to Los Angeles in twenty minutes.

Don't worry. I'm not going to tell you to be like Elon Musk. No one is like Elon Musk, except for Elon. He's one of a kind. To try and mimic him, or aspire to do what he does, is a fantastic plan if you want to become chronically depressed. What I will suggest is that you take bits and pieces of his character and emulate them. *Thinking big*, for example. By this, I don't mean you should plan on building spaceships. I mean you should expect great things from yourself.

Thinking big gives you permission to aim high. Aiming high gives you permission to make mistakes. And making mistakes allows you to learn and improve. If you simply stay within your realm of comfort, you'll never know how far your abilities can extend. So, assume you'll be able to do whatever you want. Operate in that mindset. When you fail, learn from your mistakes and put your next foot forward. Being big isn't all that important. But thinking big is critical.

THEY'RE OKAY WITH BEING SMALL

Rob Walling is a serial entrepreneur. He's been self funding his life for eleven years. He's the CEO of Drip, a company that builds email marketing tools.

He also co-hosts a conference called MicroConf and a podcast called Startups for the Rest of Us.

I've interviewed Rob personally, and he's a fantastic guy. I admire him because he's okay with being small. What I mean is he doesn't care about being the next Steve Jobs. He, in fact, prefers not to be that. He'd rather run a bootstrapped business, free from the prying hands of venture capitalists. Free from everything, really. Rob hustled to get into that position, and it's exactly where he wants to be. Hustling isn't about working your ass off until you're big. It's about creating your optimal reality—whether that's big, small, or purple.

The founders of Basecamp, Jason Fried and David Heinemeier Hansson, have a similar outlook. Here's what they say about staying small (from their book, *Rework)*:

> *"Do we look at Harvard or Oxford and say, "If they'd only expand and branch out and hire thousands more professors and go global and open other campuses all over the world ...then they'd be great schools." Of course not. That's not how we measure the value of these institutions. So why is it the way we measure businesses?"*

CHAPTER 9

THE LIFESTYLE OF A HUSTLER

This is where things get a little more advanced. If you've been hustling for a while, the stories in this chapter will sound familiar. Being a hustler is challenging. You'll get tired of it. You'll run out of ideas. You'll feel lost. Your projects will fail. At least a few friends and/or family members won't understand what you're working on, or why. When you finally complete a big project successfully, they won't care. People, in all areas of your life, will unintentionally annoy you. You won't be making enough money. The list goes on.

Don't be fooled by the catchy headlines: *"Clever Hustler Becomes Millionaire Overnight Selling Edible iPhone Cases Made of Cheese,"* or, *"MicroSlush Founder Suddenly Worth 100 Billion With New Infusion of Cash From Mystery Investor."* Sorry, that's not how it happens. If you're truly going to hustle, you need to think about it as a way of life. Just like anything else, it takes time. It has its ups and downs. This section details some of the situations you can expect, along with the mindset and practical tools that will help you live through them.

GRIND

Rich Roll is an inspiring guy. He's a plant-based nutrition enthusiast, a #1 bestselling author, and according to *Men's Fitness* magazine, one of the twenty five most fittest men in the world.

One of Rich's defining qualities is his dedication to dedication itself. He believes we live in a hack culture, where people seek to find the quickest, easiest route to success. And I agree. Hustling isn't always about hacking. It's just as much, if not more, about grinding. Here's Rich:

So if you have a passion and aspire to greatness—if you want to see what you are truly made of, or just how far you can go and what you are truly capable of—forget the hack. Commit to the daily pressure that compels infinitesimal progress over time. Wake up before dawn and apply yourself in silent anonymity. Practice your craft—in whatever shape or form that may be—late into the evening with relentless rigor. Embrace the fear. Let go of perfection. Allow yourself to fail. Welcome the obstacles. Forget the results. Give yourself over to your passion with every fiber of who you are. And live out the rest of your days trying to do better.

I can't promise that you will succeed in the way our culture inappropriately defines the term. But I can absolutely guarantee that you will become deeply acquainted with who you truly are. You will touch and exude passion. And discover what it means to be truly alive.

Before you email me to tell me this book is a hack and that I'm a hypocrite, think about it for a second. Is it? Or is it part of a longer grind?

The next time you sit down to work, think about what you're doing. Are you dedicating yourself to a craft? Are you grinding through it and honing your skills? Are you doing truly meaningful work? Hustling isn't about winning or getting paid. It's about living for your purpose.

KEEP YOUR HEAD DOWN

Jan was born in a small town outside of Kiev, Ukraine. He was an only child. His mother was a housewife, his father a construction manager. When Koum was sixteen, he and his mother immigrated to Mountain View, California, mainly to escape the anti-semitic environment of their homeland. Unfortunately, Jan's father never made the trip. He got stuck in the Ukraine, where he eventually died years later. His mother swept the floors of a grocery store to make ends meet, but she was soon diagnosed with cancer. They barely survived off her disability insurance. It certainly wasn't the most glamorous childhood, but he made it through.

After college, Jan applied to work at Yahoo as an infrastructure engineer. He spent nine years building his skills at Yahoo, and then applied to work at Facebook. Unfortunately, he was rejected. In 2009, Jan bought an iPhone and realized there was an opportunity to build something on top of Apple's burgeoning mobile platform. He began building an app that could send status updates between devices. It didn't do very well at first, but then Apple released push notifications. All of the sudden, people started getting pinged when statuses were updated. And then people began pinging back and forth. Jan realized he had inadvertently created a messaging service.

The app continued to grow, but Jan kept quiet. He didn't care about headlines or marketing buzz. He just wanted to build something valuable, and do it well. By early 2011, his app had reached the top twenty in the U.S. app store. Two years later, in 2013, the app had 200 million users. And then it happened: In 2014, Jan's company, WhatsApp, was acquired by Facebook—the company who had rejected him years earlier—for $19 billion.

I'm not telling this story to insinuate that you should go build a billion-dollar company. The remarkable part of the story isn't the payday, but the relentless hustle Jan demonstrated throughout his entire life. After surviving a tumultuous childhood, he practiced his craft and built iteratively. When had had a product that was working, he stayed quiet, which takes extreme discipline. More often than not, hustling isn't fast or showy. Most of the time it's slow and unglamorous—until it's not.

FIND YOUR MAXIMUM CONTRIBUTION

Practice makes perfect. It's true. You can't succeed without practice. But how do you know what to practice?

Some nights I can't sleep. I get out of bed and run to my computer, writing furiously—which is what I'm doing right now. I have an idea, something I think is insightful. After graduating from college, I found myself in ZombieLand. If you've read *The Connection Algorithm*, you'll know that ZombieLand is my term for a life without passion. I've done my best to escape ZombieLand. Sometimes I fall back into it momentarily, but then I claw my way back out.

When I wake up in the middle of the night and run to my computer, it's because I have an idea that I think is insightful—useful. By useful, I mean it seems beneficial to me, and therefore could be beneficial to others. It took me a long time to realize that the second part of the previous sentence is the important part: It could be beneficial to others.

For pretty much my whole life, I thought I was living to better myself, to create the best life possible. About a year ago, that mindset changed. I now believe I'm here to create the best *world* possible. This shift from *me* to *everyone* is what altered my entire understanding of passion, and my purpose.

Ben Horowitz is one of my digital mentors (meaning I follow his blog). I find him very insightful. Whenever he says (or writes about) anything, I inevitably start nodding my head until my neck is sore. Here's an excerpt from the commencement speech he gave at Columbia, his alma mater:

> *"Following your passion is a very me centered view of the world, and as you go through life, what you'll find is that what you take out of the world over time—be it...money, cars, stuff, accolades—is much less important than what you put into the world. And so my recommendation would be to follow your contribution. Find the thing that you're great at, put that into the world, contribute to others, help the world be better. That is the thing to follow."*

Most of the time, if you follow your contribution, it's either already a passion, or likely to become one. Doing something you're good at is intoxicating, as is contributing to the world. Writing and launching *The Connection Algorithm* was a full year of hard work. It was the result of countless hours of reflection, deeply philosophical thinking, and brutal honesty. Throughout the entire process, I felt driven, passionate, and motivated. At first, I thought this was because I was doing it on my own. But I've come to realize it was something else—something far more profound.

Shortly after the book was released, I began receiving emails from people who had read the book and been deeply impacted by it. A highschooler in Miami. An entrepreneur in Amsterdam. A small business owner in the midwest. People were also leaving reviews on Amazon—people I didn't know, saying the book helped them live a better life. And on my Kindle, I could see passages that people were highlighting. People weren't just reading my book, they were taking notes on useful things to remember.

The craft of writing has been unbelievably fulfilling for me. And so I'm continuing the pursuit. My motivation is no longer to make a buck, or "win at life." Rather, I'm working to improve the world. I think of myself as an inventor, creating a new piece of art for the world to discover.

When you make the world better, you get rewarded. So find your craft, and then determine the best contribution you can make with it.

The term *hustler* often conjures up images of sleazy salesman who are building up mountains of cash so they can buy the mansion or the shiny car. But I see hustlers differently. I see them as the game changers, the doers, the revolutionaries. I see them as the small few who are pushing the rest of us up the mountain, because it feels good.

KNOW WHEN TO SPRINT

Doing a project quickly doesn't mean it will be half-assed, sloppy, or unworthy. On the contrary, it often leads to a more inspired and higher-quality output. This counterintuitive outcome is the result of two common side effects of sprinting: Focus and acceleration.

When you're focused, you're more likely to get into the Zone, or *flow*. When you're in a state of flow, you do your best work. By working quickly, you also create work at an accelerated pace. This momentum generates even more flow and allows you to produce more high-quality work at a faster rate. Because you have momentum, you're less likely to become uninspired and lose your flow.

Sprinting isn't sustainable over time. You can't sprint forever. So you have to decide when to sprint, when to break, and when to coast. Should your next pursuit be a sprint or a marathon? (Tip: Sprints almost always happen inside marathons). Here are a few quick examples of how sprinting can pay dividends:

StickyNotes
This was my first startup's flagship product. It was built in less than a week. The app quickly amassed millions of users, and became the launchpad for our company.

Flappy Bird
Many will recall the simple mobile game, Flappy Bird. It was built in a few days by an independent developer in Vietnam named Dong Nguyen. In 2014, the game rose in popularity to become the most downloaded free game in the app store. At that time, Nguyen claimed the app was earning $50,000 per day in advertising revenues.

Million Dollar Baby
Clint Eastwood directed, co-produced, scored, and acted in this critically acclaimed film, which was released in 2004. It was nominated for seven acad-

emy awards, and won four, including Best Picture, and Best Director (Clint Eastwood). The film grossed over $200 million worldwide. Amazingly, it was produced for only $30 million. But even more impressive, it was filmed in just thirty seven days, which is unheard of in the movie business.

GET SHIT DONE

This book was written, designed, and published in seven days. Yes, that's right. Seven. I'll tell you how it happened.

My first book took a year to produce. It launched in May 2015 and it's performing well. It's a #1 bestseller in multiple categories on Amazon, and comes with endorsements from industry heavy-hitters like Brad Feld and Tony Horton. But after launching it, I noticed something interesting: There were other books performing just as well as mine, if not better, that didn't come with endorsements.

One such book I stumbled across was called *Book Launch*. It's by Chandler Bolt. He's 21, and he has five #1 Amazon bestsellers. He's also the CEO of Self-Publishing School, a seven-figure business that teaches people how to write, publish, and market their books. Chandler argues that anyone can write a book in 90 days with the proper planning and technique. But he also tells the story of how he and his partner wrote one of their books in only ten days. That's when the little voice in my head chimed in: *"If he can do it, so can I."*

And I did. In fact, I only needed seven. Averaging 7,000 words per day, I had 28,000 by day four, which is more than enough for a quick, punch-you-in-the-face book about hustling. I know a lot about hustle. I've lived the hustler's life for the past ten years. In my free time, I read about it. It's second nature to me. Writing a book in seven days was the perfect demonstration of a hustle project in action, and it was also the one thing I needed to focus on to enable everything else I was working on.

When you give yourself ridiculous deadlines, you find a way to hit them. In scholarly terms, this is known as Parkinson's Law. "Work expands so as to fill the time available for its completion." Getting shit done, like so many things in life, is a mindset. Refocus on what you need to do right now to keep moving forward. Then make it happen. What gets you to the next step?

SHIP PRODUCT

I'm releasing this book before I should. I haven't checked for typos. I haven't consulted with 100 beta readers. I haven't sought out endorsements or planned an elaborate launch. Some would say that's stupid. But I'm testing the market. I'm shipping product. *The Lean Startup* method praises the act of shipping early and often. You don't know what you don't know. Sometimes you don't have the ability to wait another month, or another week. You need results today.

Shipping an MVP (Minimum Viable Product) is generally accepted by consumers in today's marketplace. Early adopters understand that products are often released in beta form. They can handle a few hiccups as long as you work to fix them. If you have a suggestion that could help me improve this book, let me know: jesse.tevelow@gmail.com. I'll happily consider your feedback.

FIGHT IN THE TRENCHES

My store, Wine Library, outsells big national chains. How do you think we do it? It started with hustle." —Gary Vaynerchuk

Hustlers don't watch from the sidelines. They get in the game. They get their hands dirty. Tim Cook, the CEO of Apple, is notorious for responding to customer emails. Much like Steve Jobs before him, he realizes the importance of being in the trenches. This isn't a publicity stunt. It's a chance for Cook to learn what his customers like and don't like. It's an opportunity for him to feel the customer's pain. Without going straight to the source, you can't get that kind of insight.

KEEP ON HUSTLING

Noah Kagan went to UC Berkeley and graduated with degrees in Business and Economics. He worked at Intel for a short stint, and then found himself at Facebook, as employee #30. You'd think this is where the story would get really good: *Noah went on to become the head of product and is now worth 10 billion dollars!* That's not what happened. Instead, he was fired after eight months. Noah has been very public about this, and it's well documented. He even wrote about why it happened, which mostly comes down to the fact that he was young and inexperienced.

Here's where the real story gets interesting. After being fired, Noah spent ten months at Mint, another successful startup. For Noah, that was a side-hustle. After Mint, he founded KickFlip, a payment provider for social games. He also started an ad company called Gambit. Both of those companies fluttered around for a while and then fizzled out. Next came AppSumo, a daily deals website for tech software. AppSumo has done very well, and it's still in business as of this writing, but Noah eventually turned his attention to another opportunity.

While building up his other businesses, he had become an expert at email marketing, and realized there was a huge need for effective marketing tools. So he created SumoMe, a software company that helps people and companies build their email lists.

SumoMe has exploded since its launch. Over 200,000 sites now use it in some capacity, and that number is growing every day. It's easy to imagine SumoMe becoming a $100 million dollar company in a matter of years, and it's completely bootstrapped. The company has taken zero funding from venture capitalists. That means Noah can run the business exactly how he wants.

I've known Noah for almost ten years. I met him when my first company was getting off the ground. Several months ago, we were emailing back and forth about promoting my first book. He ended one of the emails with, "Keep the hustle strong." I smiled when I read that. Noah is, and always will be, a hustler. He's been hustling for his entire career—for over a decade. And he deserves everything that's coming his way. Hustle never comes without defeat. It never comes without detours and side-projects. But the best hustlers all know this simple truth: All that matters is that you keep on hustling.

CHAPTER 10

THIRTY-SIX HOURS OF PURE FOCUS

I t's been nearly thirty-six hours since I first de-cided to do this crazy experiment. I'm feeling a little dizzy. But I'm also feeling excited. Here are a few things I've learned after writing a full book draft in three days:

1. *The rules can be re-written.* When you set ridiculous constraints, you can achieve ri-diculous things. It forces you to get organized and act. Things don't take as long as you think they do. I thought it would be impossible to write 30,000 words in three days, but I made it happen. (To be com-pletely honest, I didn't quite hit the mark. I'm at 24K. Maybe 30K is truly impossible. Kidding.) Over the past three days I've also

worked out every day, cooked almost every meal I ate, and slept about eight hours a night.

2. *It's NOT overwhelming.* Ironically, it's not overwhelming because you can see what's in front of you. Planning a seven day project is easier than planning a seven month project. Compressing a substantial project into a short period of time is like ripping off a bandaid vs. slowly peeling it off. It's not that painful if you just brace yourself and yank it.

3. *Working faster = More focus, passion, and output*—not lower quality, as one might expect.

4. *You'll still have time for breaks.* As I mentioned, I ate meals, cleaned, and worked out every day. Which, in turn, improved my writing.

5. *It's invigorating.* I haven't felt this alive in a long time. It's like being in a high-speed chase. That alone is worth the experience.

6. *Sometimes gems emerge from full immersion.* Doing something crazy every once in awhile is a surprisingly effective way to stumble into greatness. It gets you out of your normal thought patterns and leads to breakthroughs.

7. *You have to make sacrifices.* If you take this approach, you'll need to cut certain things out of your plan. I knew I wouldn't be able to do much research, so I stuck to what I already knew. No time for interviews. The initial version of the book won't have the best design, either. And there will likely be some typos. But that's okay.

8. *Working fast affects the aura of your product.* When you work fast, you think fast. When you think fast, you write fast. When you write fast, you write in simple terms. The tone and pace of the book feels fast and intense because I wrote it that way—which ended up being a good thing.

9. *I need to invest in a better chair.* My back hurts like hell.

What does this all mean?

In a nutshell, this is repeatable. You can do it, too. Based on the pace I achieved, it's conceivable that you could write a book within any of the following timeframes:

- A single three-day weekend.

- One week, if you spend six hours each night OR three hours in the morning and three at night.
- One month, if you dedicate each Sunday OR just one hour per day.

The above examples get you a finished draft. Then you'll need at least a few more days for editing and design, plus another 1-2 weeks for a pre-release buildup before officially launching. With any of these approaches, your content will probably come out better than if you were to space it out over a year or more. It also means you can apply the same principles to whatever else you want to accomplish. It means you don't have to start your hustling journey with an epic quest. You can start with a sprint instead.

Counterpoints: Of course, this isn't the best approach for every book. It's not the best idea if:

- You want to write a lengthy book
- You want to interview people
- You need to do a bunch of research
- You want to publish with a traditional publisher

Obviously the system won't work for every project outside of books, either.

CHAPTER 11

HUSTLER'S DIARY - DAY 4

Saturday, December 12th 2015

6 a.m. To be honest, I lost momentum last night. After staring at my computer for nearly two hours without writing a sentence, I gave up and went to bed around 11. Luckily, I woke up this morning feeling refreshed. Sometimes you just need to let yourself breathe. You can't force the action. I love going to bed because I know the next morning will be a new start—a new opportunity. And when you're in the middle of an intense project, your mind naturally jumps to that project when your eyelids swing open. I leapt out of bed with incredible energy at 5 a.m. After going through my normal early morning routine, I started writing.

Today is supposed to be the beginning of Phase 2—edits, design, and launch prep—but I still haven't reached the 30K mark, so I wanted to get a few thousand additional words in. I found that my writing pace slowed each day. I started with 10K, then 8K, then 6K—which put me at a total of 24K. That pattern makes sense. It's easy to write a lot when nothing has been written yet. Thinking about it in those logical terms makes me feel better. After an hour of writing this morning, I'm now at 26,000 words.

I know I'll be adding more content once I go through the editing process and devise my launch plan. The strategy for launch will be worked into the book as well, so I might hit 30K after that's added in. Hitting 30K isn't all that important though, to be honest. It's just an arbitrary milestone. At this stage, I'll be focusing more on the quality of the content. If the best possible product happens to top out at 28K, that's fine. Or, maybe it will be 35K. It always comes down to quality, not quantity. I never look at data alone to make decisions. I also put my gut into the equation. As a hustler, you have to be able to feel what the market wants. I'll be working primarily on Phase 2 for the rest of the day. Looking forward to getting into it.

FROM CONCEPT TO LAUNCH IN 7 DAYS

I created the blueprint below so you can under-stand exactly how a hustle project comes together. But I also created it for my own benefit, so *I* had a blueprint to follow. This is a perfect example of combining efficiency and effectiveness.

If you don't plan on writing a book in seven days, you can skip this section. However, the general principles of any hustle project are the same, so you may still find it useful. Taylor Pearson has a great brain dump on writing, launching, and marketing a book as well. If you have a longer timeline than seven days, you should check out his approach. Just google: "Taylor Pearson Jesus Marketing" and it will pop right up. Here's my process for a seven-day book:

PHASE	TASKS	DAYS
1	Outline, write, small edits	3
2	Major edits, book design, launch prep	3
3	Publish	1

Phase 1: Outline, Write, Small Edits

1. *Choose your software.* Google Docs is my word processing software of choice.
2. *Create an outline within your manuscript using the TOC feature.* I love Google Docs because it has an amazing Table of Contents feature. The TOC is created automatically

based on how you format your document. If you're having trouble figuring this out, email me (jesse.tevelow@gmail.com) and I'll send you a template. By using this feature, the TOC doubles as your outline—which makes it very easy to visualize the book's overarching structure. Build out the outline a little, until you have enough to start writing. Then add to the outline as you go. It will be easier to fill in the gaps as you write.

3. *Use a Train of Thought document.* When you're writing super fast, your mind will dart around. Random, but relevant, ideas will jump into your head. When this happens, you have to be ready to capture them. I use a separate document titled Train of Thought for this situation. When an idea strikes, I jump into my TOT doc and start writing. I use it only for immediate brain dumping that doesn't fit into the existing outline. Once I've dumped it all down, I polish it and find a place for it in the actual manuscript document. If there isn't a good spot, I'll create a new section for it.

4. *Track your pace.* The pacing goal is 1,000 words per hour (continuous goal), and

10,000 words per day (end goal). Check your word count as you write. My pace slowed with each day, and yours might too, but that's okay. Starting with a high daily goal will ensure you start off strong. My pattern was 10K, 8K, 6K, 4K—for a total of 28K.

5. *Use dictation.* Google Docs has a dictation feature. Simply allow Google to access your computer's internal mic, and you can speak your book. The words will appear on the page as you speak. You can also easily type edits as you go. When I hit a writing block, this sometimes helps. It's a good way to shake things up.

6. *Make only small edits.* During the three-day sprint, you should be writing quickly, and writing a lot. There should be minimal editing. Throughout the day, go back through your content to make small corrections to grammar, wording, punctuation, etc. But be disciplined. If you find yourself making broader structural or conceptual changes, stop yourself. That will come in Phase 2.

Phase 2: Major Edits, Book Design, Launch Prep

Major Edits:

1. After the writing sprint is over (Days 1-3), refer to the outline (i.e. Table of Contents) for big structural changes that could improve flow. Cut entire chapters if they suck. Move sections around.

2. Read the book aloud to yourself over and over again, making updates along the way whenever a sentence sounds awkward.

3. Use the TOC to identify new chapters that could enhance the book's overall message. If you think of anything new, write it out, and add it in.

4. Re-work your intro. Your intro is the most important section of the book. Spend time on this.

5. Once the ordering of the book is feeling good, go back through and write transitions between chapters and sections to improve the flow even further.

Book Design:

1. *Interior Design*: You can use bookdesign-templates.com for your interior book

design. This service comes recommended by Joanna Penn from the Creative Penn (Google her). Joanna is highly regarded in the self-publishing space, and I recently had the opportunity to do an interview with her. She knows her stuff. *Tip:* Befriend people in your field. Consult with them, or email a few experts for advice. This is often more effective than blindly searching the internet for resources.

2. *Exterior Cover Design:* I'll be using the cover elements from my first book, *The Connection Algorithm*, and editing them in Photoshop to create a new cover. This will give my books a consistent look, which is a plus from both an efficiency and effectiveness standpoint. *Tip:* Reuse content that works. I'm lucky since I already released a book and have some existing materials. This is an example of building iterative value—grinding. If you don't already have existing material, bookdesigntemplates.com has cover templates. You can also try CreateSpace (Amazon's self-publishing arm), 99designs, or Fiverr.

Launch Prep:

1. *Set up GumRoad and Amazon.* Because I'm writing and publishing this book in seven days, I have to get creative. The process is rushed, to say the least. To give myself a safety cushion, I'm planning to set up both Amazon (platform) and Gumroad (direct pay). I will likely use one or the other on launch day.

2. *Create ThunderClap Campaign.* Thunderclap is a clever service that allows friends to easily participate in product launches. Friends who agree to take part essentially pledge to broadcast a pre-written message on social media on the day of the launch. At the specified time, Thunderclap automatically posts the message from everyone's pre-approved social networks, creating a 'surround-sound' effect across the social web. I haven't used it before, but I've heard great things.

3. *Compile all contact lists.* I reached out to various contact groups for the launch of my first book (including Kickstarter backers, fraternity alumni, and my general email account). Since then, I've also built up a small but loyal email list from my website, and

grown a private Facebook group to about 120 members. I'll need to organize these lists and start emailing them once the Thunderclap campaign is setup. I don't want to just blurt out the news at the last second. As Jeff Walker has demonstrated by popularizing the Sideways Sales letter, it's better to build a story around a product launch over time, vs. launching with one big announcement and no warning. Even though I'm planning to publish on Day 7 (December 15th), I may need to push the Thunderclap date to January 4th. It would be ideal to do the launch promo closer to the publish date, but I'm doing this right around Christmas, so it's a little tricky.

4. *Draft emails.* I'll draft emails to my lists on Sunday (Day 5) so they'll be ready to go out when I launch. Because I already have a great story about how this project came about, it should be easy to make the email interesting.

5. *Copywriting for Sales Page.* To create the copy for the sales pages on Amazon and Gumroad, I'll modify the text I'm planning to use on the back cover of the book. If I run into any snags, I'll look at examples of

similar top-selling books on Amazon for inspiration.

Phase 3: Publish

Launch day is set for Day 7, which is Tuesday, December 15th. When I say, "launch," keep in mind
I'm talking about a soft launch—meaning the book
will be available for purchase on Amazon or Gumroad, but I won't promote it. The official launch will
likely come 1-3 weeks later, since I'm doing this
around the holidays. During this waiting period, I'll
collect reviews from friends to create social proof,
and keep gathering supporters for my Thunderclap
campaign.

It's preferable to do the official launch on a
Sunday. Launching on Sunday gives me one day to
gain some steam before the week starts. If I use
Amazon, I'll be enrolling in their KDP program,
which allows me to set the book's price to *free* for
five days. I'll plan for the Thunderclap campaign to
hit on Monday (day two of free promo). If this
works, I should be able to get a healthy amount of
downloads on Sunday while I make sure everything
is working properly, and then climb the charts on
Monday when the Thunderclap message drops.
Getting free sales is useful because it increases visi-

bility when the book switches from *free* to *paid*. I
know this from my last book launch.

CHAPTER 13

HUSTLER'S DIARY - DAY 5

Sunday, December 13th, 2015

7:30 a.m. I had an epiphany this morning. It struck, of course, while I was doing the dishes. I'll get back to that in a moment. First, I want to tell you about the rest of Day 4.

Yesterday was highly productive, but probably the hardest day so far. I spent about half my time editing the book (mainly structural updates, moving sections around, etc.), and half my time working on production (researching interior book design options, creating the book's front and back covers, graphics, etc.). I've come to realize that the production and promotion aspects of the product lifecycle are far more challenging and time con-

suming than creating the product itself. I actually already knew this from my experience in the startup world, and from books like Traction, by Gabriel Weinberg and Justin Mares—but it's hitting me like a load of bricks now that I'm in the thick of it again.

Today, I need to complete the book in its entirety. That means I need to read it aloud to myself as many times as possible, diligently remove content that isn't substantive or relevant, add any last-minute material, and polish everything that's already there. That's a lot to do in a single day. But that's not all. I also need to convert the entire book into its final digital and print-ready formats so I can submit it to Amazon for processing. It sometimes takes several days for Amazon to send a proof, and I want to make sure the paperback is ready for sale by the time I officially launch.

Because Amazon needs the final version in order to review it, process it, and send the proof—I need to 'freeze' the book today. That means no more edits or additional content. And so, this will be the final diary entry. The rest of next week will be entirely focused on marketing efforts. I'll be reaching out to my family, friends, and fans (the 'FFF Approach'...I like that as an acronym) to build buzz and get early reviews. In parallel, I'll be set-

ting up other marketing tools like Thunderclap to
ensure I'm ready for launch day. If the details of
the creation and launch process are interesting to
you, you're in luck. I'll be releasing a much more
in-depth book about this called The Dawn of Books
after Hustle is done. To get an early free copy of it,
just go to my website, (www.jtev.me) and join my
mailing list. Before signing off, here's the epiphany
I had while doing the dishes:

Momentum is everything. Momentum creates inspiration, which leads to high-quality production.
This is why standing still equates to imminent failure, and making moves guarantees eventual
success. It's literally that simple. Even more en-
couraging: The more momentum you generate, the
higher the probability of **monumental** success. I
hadn't realized it until now, but this is the crux of
the book. It's the entire purpose.

I created a graphic for my cover last night—
two curved arrows forming a circle, demonstrating a continuous cycle. I didn't know it at the time,
but it perfectly captures the self-perpetuating system of hustling. It gives me great joy to know that
I've stumbled across such a crystallized explana-
tion of what I've been writing about for the past
several days. I hope you find it valuable, too. If you

take anything away from this book, remember to never stop moving. And now, on with Day 5. Farewell, J

CHAPTER 14

SO YOU WANT TO BE A HUSTLER

If you want to hustle, you have to live your life as a hustler. You can't just want it, or do it once or twice. You have to be doing it all the time. That might sound trivial, but it's not. Most people talk about it, but don't take action. This chapter focuses on some of the major steps you can take to truly live the hustler's life. It also includes a final wrap-up about the mindset you should be aiming for, and the motivations that should be driving you. Let's start by looking at how to remove doubt and toxic relationships.

REMOVE ALL DOUBT

> "It's easy to give in to your fear and tell yourself that you don't have what it takes to lead. Mostly, people give up when they get to the charisma part of the checklist. "I wasn't born charismatic, not like those other guys, so I guess I'll just settle for following." The flaw in this reasoning is that those other guys weren't born charismatic either. It's a choice, not a gift."
>
> - Seth Godin, Tribes

Self doubt is a virus. It can seep into your soul and infect your entire being. While self doubt is by definition a self-inflicted condition, it's actually caused by destructive relationships. Destructive relationships plant seeds of doubt within your mind, over and over again. When these seeds have time to fester, it's very difficult to remove them.

If you can identify relationships that are contributing to your self doubt, you've taken the first step in fixing the problem. The second step is to eradicate those relationships. There's no room for self doubt in your life. It is the single biggest threat to your growth and happiness.

REMOVE TOXIC RELATIONSHIPS

A toxic relationship is a relationship that stifles your productivity and gets in the way of your hustle. Growth can be blocked by many things, but common culprits include psychological abuse, constant unnecessary mental interruptions, and bad habits that degrade your health. Be careful when defining positive versus negative interactions within a relationship. It's sometimes difficult to discern constructive criticism from destructive criticism.

Many of us, including myself, are bad at identifying positive versus negative relationships. This is the real challenge. How many times have you, or someone you know, continued a relationship for far too long before cutting if off? It happens all the time because:

1. Most of us don't want to admit that a relationship is bad after we've spent the time and energy building it.

2. Most of us can't find a way to be confident in our decision to finally let a relationship go. The longer the relationship lasts, the harder it is to cut it off.

I've fallen victim to this for nearly my whole life. I have a tendency to hold on until the world comes crumbling down. This is precisely what we want to avoid. While it's never black and white, I've developed a few exercises to make the decision a little easier.

1. The Short Form Toxicity Test
2. The Long Form Toxicity Test
3. The Gut Toxicity Test

The Short Form Toxicity Test

If you think there is a questionable relationship in your life (be honest with yourself), I encourage you to try this exercise. If and when you try it, it's important that you follow the steps exactly. Here's how it works:

Find a relaxed time to do the exercise. It shouldn't be done during a time of heightened or abnormal emotion. For example, you shouldn't do the exercise immediately after a big fight, or during a vacation. It should be done when your state of mind is normal and calm. When you're ready, follow these steps:

1. Find a quiet place where you can think clearly. Bring a timer with you. Use the timer in the steps that follow.

2. Take two minutes to think about the relationship in question. Think about how that person interacts with you, and all the various things you do together.

3. For the next five minutes, write these interactions down, as well as how the interactions make you feel, in this exact format: "When [name] does _____, it makes me feel _____". Let these statements flow onto the page as naturally and as quickly as possible. You should record statements as they pop into your head and try not to think too long between each one.

4. Continue this process until you have at least ten statements. You can write more if you want, but you need at least ten. Don't spend more than five minutes on this.

5. After the five minutes are up, go back through your list and put a +1 or -1 next to each statement, based on the feeling you expressed at the end of each sentence. Posi-

tive feelings get a +1, while negative feelings get a -1. For example, if the emotion is *frustrated* you would record a -1, and if the emotion is *happy* you would record a +1.

6. Multiply statement 1 by five and statement 2 by two.
7. Sum the values of all statements.
8. Subtract 1 to get your total score.

If the total score is negative, you should be thinking seriously about cutting the relationship out of your life. If the total score is positive, you should keep the relationship intact. The further away you are from zero, the stronger the indication for keeping or cutting someone. For example, a score of -1 is a weaker indicator than a score of -10, and conversely a score of +1 is weaker than a score of +10.

Statements one and two are multiplied by five and two respectively because they are far more important than the others. The first thought out of your head is a huge indicator of how you really feel. Is your initial thought about the person positive or negative? If it's negative, you likely have a big problem. Step 8 is included because if you're doing the test in the first place, you already doubt the relationship on a subconscious level—even if you don't realize it.

All that really matters is how the person makes you feel on average. The relationship either fuels or saps your confidence, happiness, and everything else that gives you the strength to be the best you can be. If these feelings are being undermined, the person needs to be removed from your life as quickly as possible.

Long Form Toxicity Test
While the Short Form Toxicity Test is quick and easy, it's partially flawed. You'll most likely skew the results by accident. Because you know the purpose of the test in advance, you may subconsciously sugarcoat things, leave things out, or balance your negative comments with positive ones. Your emotions essentially won't be authentic. The long form approach takes longer, but it can provide a more accurate reading.

The long form test uses the same method as the short form test, but you will track emotions daily for a period of 2-4 weeks instead of recording them in a single session. You should also include one or more additional people in the test if possible. You should choose people who are close to you and interact with you frequently.

The added elements of this test (recording your emotions in real time, extending the duration, and adding more people) all contribute to the authenticity of the results. The real-time nature will ensure your thoughts are fresh and accurate. Doing the test over multiple days with multiple people will prevent you from subconsciously rigging the results. It's harder to keep track of the proportion of negative to positive comments attributed to a single person with the added elements of time and multiple subjects, so instead of subconsciously keeping a pulse on how negative or positive you're being, you'll be more likely to record raw emotion. The results will only become clear when you tabulate everything later.

With the long form approach, you don't need to do Step 6 from the short form test. Each emotion simply gets a +1 or -1. Don't add the numbers until the four week period ends. If there are instances when people contribute little or nothing to your mood, there's no need to record anything on those days.

The Gut Toxicity Test

The Gut Toxicity Test isn't really a test, but it's effective if you can execute it. It's the easiest and fastest of the three approaches, but the most difficult to act on because there's no hard data. Essentially, your gut already knows what to do. If you're questioning a relationship, it's likely bad. If you can trust your gut and take action, you'll usually be glad you did.

Don't take these tests lightly. If the score from your Short Form or Long Form test is very negative (-5 or lower), you should consider it urgent. This person could be your boss, a close friend, or even a family member.

It may seem impossible to cut ties with such important people in your life. Trust me, you need to do it. It will be hard, but it's necessary. The other person may express a desire to fix things in some cases. I would still recommend cutting off the relationship. Coming back to it later is certainly an option, but in most cases, mending a battered relationship without an extended break in between is extremely difficult.

A few final thoughts and tips:

We all have to deal with people we don't like. We're looking for the biggest offenders in relation to your growth. If your boss or your best friend is causing you great pain, you need to consider changing your life in a major way. Conversely, if you don't like your mailman, learn to deal with it and get on with your day.

Destroy the evidence. Saving these tests to your desktop is a bad idea. If you choose to maintain ties with someone after taking the test, and that person happens to find the results, it can sabotage the relationship that you had planned to keep intact. Discard the information promptly after getting your results.

Just because a relationship is toxic doesn't mean either person involved is evil. It just means the two people are not aligned. There are certain personalities that don't mesh well together. The important thing to realize is that bad relationships aren't productive. So, get out. Don't hold a grudge against the other person and don't judge them. Just realize that things aren't working and move on. You'll both be happier. It's a win-win.

DON'T TRY TO FIGURE IT ALL OUT

Hustlers have a laser focus. They know what they need to do next. Ask them what they need to do ten steps down the road, and they'll have no answer for you. This is a good thing. As I've mentioned, the problem with long lists is that they inevitably change.

Write down a one-year plan. I dare you to follow it. Even a six-month plan is too far out. I operate a few months at a time. That doesn't mean I don't have long-term goals or an idea of where I want to go. I'm just aware that I can't plan every step out that far with any accuracy. It's better to plan a few steps, work on them, plan a few more, work on those, and so on.

I use Asana to manage my work. It acts as my To-Do list. Asana allows me to put tasks in three categories: *Today, Upcoming,* and *Later.* On most days, I move 1-3 items into the *Today* section. Those are the things I want to get done that day, or that week. *Upcoming* holds most everything else. And *Later* just has big ideas or stuff I don't really care about. That's it. I don't try to figure everything out. I know that my schedule will change based on the results of the things I'm working on in the short term.

TAKE A CHANCE

> *"You have to struggle a bit, hustle a little, and be willing to go bankrupt. Once you're*

> *willing to do that, everything opens up and*
> *you get the freedom." —Nick Nolte*

If you're hustling, you can't play it safe all the time. You have to throw the long ball every once in awhile. This book is a shot in the dark. Writing, producing, and publishing a book in seven days is a tall order. Just reading that last sentence makes me cringe in fear. But here I am, writing.

Take a moment to identify a task you're scared of doing. It should be something you know could help you a lot, but you're nervous about doing it. We all have those things on a list inside our minds. Why aren't you doing them? I can almost guarantee the inaction is caused by some form of fear. Resolve right now to put at least one of those lingering items on your to-do list tomorrow. Take action on it. Do something to move that one thing forward.

PUT ONE FOOT AFTER THE OTHER

At the end of the first P90X DVD, Tony Horton casually offers some amazing advice. His words are simple, but profound: "Keep pushing play." He's talking about putting the DVD into the DVD player. "Just show up," he says.

The P90X workouts are admittedly hard, but you're guaranteed to fail if you never even push the play button. *Play* is also a great word. In this context, I view it as starting. Activating yourself. Enjoying yourself. Pushing yourself. Experiencing the struggle and enjoying it. When you're trying to improve (physically, mentally, spiritually, or otherwise), remember to keep pushing play. You don't have to be the best to be successful. You just have to put one foot in front of the other. Keep showing up.

NEVER GIVE UP

Jimmy Valvano was a legendary college basketball coach and broadcaster. In June of 1992, he was diagnosed with metastatic cancer. In March of the following year, Jimmy gave a powerful speech at the first ever ESPY awards, presented by ESPN. His message was just as simple as it was moving: "Don't give up. Don't ever give up." Eight weeks later, he passed away. In his speech, he also said this:

To me, there are three things we all should do every day. We should do this every day of our lives. Number one is laugh. You should laugh every day. Number two is think. You should spend some time in thought. And number three is, you should have your emotions moved to tears—could be happiness or joy. But think about it. If you laugh, you think, and you cry, that's a full day. That's a heck of a day. You do that seven days a week, you're going to have something special.

And finally, this:

Cancer can take away all of my physical abilities. It cannot touch my mind, it cannot touch my heart, and it cannot touch my soul. And those three things are going to carry on forever.

There is no other reason to be alive than to enjoy it. So laugh, think, cry. Work hard. Celebrate your victories. Embrace the day. And don't ever give up.

THE ONLY THREE THINGS THAT MATTER

I published the following passage on my personal blog on 11/26/2015, two weeks before I started writing *Hustle*.

Today is Thanksgiving, but it's also my birthday. I'm 33 years old. It's strange to say that. It feels like it should be 13 or 23. But it's 33.

I lost my father to cancer a few months ago. Watching his decline was devastating. A few months before that, my first book, *The Connection Algorithm*, was released. That project turned out to be one of the most fulfilling endeavors of my life.

I'm glad my father was here for it. For the past six months, I've been working on my second book. My emotions have been up and down with it—but lately it's feeling really good. I'm interviewing some incredible people and learning a lot. It's interesting work.

As I reflect on my father's death and the number 33 on this day of giving thanks, I can't help but ponder my own existence. I'm admittedly still grappling to find my way—to understand where I best fit. I'm far from mastering this thing called life, but here are a few things that seem to matter. In fact, they might be the only three things:

1. *Well-Being/Freedom.* I need to protect my health and my time. Time is the only non-renewable resource. Good health (meaning physical, mental, and spiritual well-being) maximizes the value of my time, while bad health renders it useless. Without time and health, I have nothing.

2. *Passion.* I'm happiest when I maximize my contribution to the world, while preserving freedom (independence). Maximized contribution means purpose. I have yet to balance purpose with financial stability. This goal seems reasonable, yet unattaina-

ble at times. While I often wonder if I'm fighting the wrong fight, I can't imagine any other way to live. I'll battle relentlessly to make this equation work—even if I die trying. Regardless of the outcome, the act of *reaching* is better than settling for anything less.

3. *Love.* Life is meaningless without relationships. There are people who make me feel good, and people who make me feel bad. It's damaging to engage with the latter—but being alone is just as tragic. It's critical to surround myself with joy, love, and support. That said, I shouldn't be afraid to welcome new people into my life. I should assume people are good. Unfortunately, I can't hold onto my loved-ones forever. I'll lose some, if not all of them, before it's my turn to go. So, I must cherish my relationships while I have them—one moment at a time.

When my father stopped breathing, my emotions oscillated between anger and gratitude: Anger that he was gone so soon; gratitude that I was able to share a significant portion of my life with him. My dad helped me understand the importance of the three pursuits above: well-being, passion, and love.

I'll never forget the special moments with him—singing in the car, hiking through the woods, and shooting hoops until dusk. Simply interacting with him was a gift. And maybe that's the point. We don't need much.

This past week, I was lucky enough to have a special birthday dinner. About ten of my local friends were there, along with my mother, who was in town from the opposite coast. It was the best birthday celebration I can remember in recent memory. I don't normally like birthdays—probably because I tend to get very reflective, and sometimes negative, about who I am and where I'm going in life. But this was different. This was simply a celebration, just for me.

It was a random Tuesday night, but my friends made the time. One of them drove two hours in traffic. Another couple, who are notoriously always late, showed up early. My mother, meeting many of my friends for the first time, had a blast. She told me afterwards, "They're all great people." And she's right. Each and every one of them is uniquely intelligent, good-natured, and a joy to be around.

I'm very fortunate. My brain works and my body works. I'm doing passionate work. And I'm surrounded by amazing people who enrich my life. I sincerely hope I do the same for them.

I'll be spending this Thanksgiving (and the actual calendar day of my birth) alone, but I'm okay with that. In a way, it will allow me to spend it with my father. I'll be watching plenty of football, as he would have done. And as the days roll by, I'll keep striving to live intentionally—because a passive life is a pointless life. I'm not sure what we're all doing here on this spinning rock, but if I had to choose something, I'd go with this quote, which I've used before:

> *"I finally figured out the only reason to be alive is to enjoy it."*
>
> —Rita Mae Brown

Sometimes I go outside and close my eyes. I look up at the sun and let its warmth hit my eyelids. Then I take a deep breath, and smile.

WHY DO YOU HUSTLE?

I hustle because climbing mountains is a hell of a lot more rewarding than stuffing envelopes. I hustle because taking chances makes my heart pump. I hustle because I want to change people's lives for the better. But most of all, I hustle so I'll be prepared for a specific moment in time, a moment we all have in common—a moment my father experienced just a few months ago: The last breath. I hustle so that when I'm exhaling in that moment, I'll be able to whisper with the sincerest of confidence, "I've given everything I can to this world. I'm at peace with my life, and so I'm at peace with death. I'm ready for the next adventure. Let's do this."

Why do you hustle? Let the world know by tweeting with the hashtag #ihustlecuz. And remember: Never stop moving. This life is precious.

CHAPTER 15

WHO ARE THE HUSTLERS?

B elow is a list of amazing hustlers. Most of them you'll recognize, some—maybe not. Look them up and see what they're about. They might inspire you. Every hustler needs a little motivation to keep the momentum churning. Of course there are countless others not listed here. Got an idea for someone who could be added to the list? Tweet at me (@jtevelow) with the hashtag #HustleList, and I'll consider including them in future updates.

THE HUSTLE LIST

Albert Einstein, Benjamin Franklin, Bill Gates, Chandler Bolt, Charles Darwin, David Heinemeier Hansson, Daymond John, Elon Musk, Frank Lloyd Wright, Gary Vaynerchuk, Halle Berry, James Altucher, Jamie Foxx, Jan Koum, Jane Austen, Jason Fried, JayZ, John Lee Dumas, Joshua Fields Millburn and Ryan Nicodemus, Ludwig van Beethoven, Magic Johnson, Mark Zuckerberg, Manny Pacquiao, Pablo Picasso, Maya Angelou, Noah Kagan, Oprah Winfrey, Pat Flynn, Rob Walling, Seth Godin, Sigmund Freud, Sophia Amoruso, Stephen Curry, Steve Jobs, Tim Ferriss, Tom Brady, Tom Hanks, Usain Bolt, Vincent van Gogh...

Who will be next? Maybe *you.*

Bonus Gift #1

THE HUSTLER'S TOOLBOX—59 RESOURCES TO HELP YOU GET YOUR HUSTLE ON

There are endless tools and resources for taking your hustle to the next level. Here are some of my favorites, ranging from software, to books, to health products, and more.

Information Synthesis
- Feedly (www.feedly.com)
- ProductHunt (www.producthunt.com)
- Medium (www.medium.com)
- HackerNews (www.news.ycombinator.com)
- Amazon Books (Create a wish list and read the intro samples)

Writing
- Google Docs (www.google.com/docs/about)
- Medium (www.medium.com)

Organization and Project Management
- Asana (www.asana.com)
- Basecamp (www.basecamp.com)
- Toggl (www.toggl.com)
- RescueTime (www.rescuetime.com)

Payments / Fundraising

- Gumroad (www.gumroad.com)
- Kickstarter (www.kickstarter.com)
- IndieGogo (www.indigogo.com)

Marketing

- Leadpages (www.leadpages.net)
- Drip (www.getdrip.com)
- ConvertKit (www.convertkit.com)
- Unbounce (www.unbounce.com)
- Appsumo (www.appsumo.com)
- SumoMe (www.sumome.com)

Designing / Prototyping

- Invision (www.invisionapp.com)
- PhotoShop (www.photoshop.com)
- Sketch (www.sketchapp.com)

Communication

- Skype (www.skype.com)
- Slack (www.slack.com)

Health

- Pull-up bar: (http://tinyurl.com/9vyclu)
- Bands: (http://tinyurl.com/zfch4le)
- Mat: (http://tinyurl.com/869ao89)
- P90X: (http://tinyurl.com/jry7sd6)

- Water Bottle: (http://tinyurl.com/zs2d9uy)
- Headspace (https://www.headspace.com/)
- Calm app (search the app store)

Podcast Recording

- Microphone: (http://tinyurl.com/6q5kdww)
- Recording: (http://www.ecamm.com/)
- Skype: (www.skype.com)

Books

- *The Four Hour WorkWeek* by Timothy Ferriss
- *The One Thing* by Gary Keller
- *The Lean Startup* by Eric Ries
- *Ready, Fire, Aim* by Michael Masterson
- *The End of Jobs* by Taylor Pearson
- *The Hard Thing about Hard Things* by Ben Horowitz
- *The Startup of You* by Ben Casnocha and Reid Hoffman
- *Daily Rituals* by Mason Currey
- *The Art of Work* by Jeff Goins
- *The War of Art* by Steven Pressfield
- *Rework* by Jason Fried and David Heinemeier Hansson
- *The Dip* by Seth Godin
- *Permission Marketing* by Seth Godin

- *Traction* by Justin Mares and Gabriel Weinberg
- *Zero to One* by Peter Thiel
- *On the Shortness of Life* by Seneca
- *The Personal MBA* by Josh Kaufman

Podcasts
- Startup
- The Tim Ferriss Show
- Entrepreneur on Fire

Self Learning
- Udemy (www.udemy.com)
- Team Treehouse (www.teamtreehouse.com)
- Codeacademy (www.codeacademy.com)
- Codesmith (www.codesmith.io)

Bonus Gift #2

My very first book, *The Connection Algorithm*, was self-published. It's now a #1 bestseller on track to generate $20,000 per year in passive income. Other part-time authors are doing far better than me, earning six, or even seven figures per year. Here's the best part: We're not writing because we have to. *We're writing because we want to*. This wasn't possible ten years ago, but the publishing industry has changed. People are finding unparalleled freedom and wealth through writing, and you can too. My forthcoming book, *The Dawn of Books*, will show you how.

If you've ever dreamt of using your knowledge for more than just a paycheck, *The Dawn of Books* is for you. And you're in luck, because you can reserve a pre-release copy **at no cost** by visiting www.jtev.me and joining my mailing list. It's honestly that simple. No strings attached.

The Dawn of Books will change the way you think about writing, but it will also prepare you to thrive in the entrepreneurial era we find ourselves in (even if you don't want to become a fulltime author). To give you unparalleled insight into the world of publishing and entrepreneurship, I've spent the past year conducting in-depth interviews with some of the industry's best and brightest. Here's a sampling:

- **Brad Feld** Author of the Startup Revolution series, managing director of Foundry Group (over $1 billion under management).
- **Taylor Pearson** Amazon #1 bestselling author of The End of Jobs.
- **Rob Walling** Founder and CEO of Drip, serial entrepreneur, author, podcaster.
- **Rohit Bhargava** Wallstreet Journal bestselling author of five business books, founder of Influential Marketing Group.
- **Chandler Bolt** 21 year old entrepreneur, running a seven-figure business for self-publishing. Author of five bestselling books on Amazon.
- **Simon Whistler** Creator of Rocking-Self Publishing, a popular podcast that explores the world of self-published books.

...just to name a few.

Are you curious about the benefits of writing a book, but too overwhelmed to get started? I can relate. I made plenty of poor choices with my first book, and wasted thousands of dollars. *The Dawn of Books* demystifies the process so you can avoid those same mistakes.

Inside, you'll find various tools and techniques you can use to guarantee a polished manuscript, a timely launch, and maximized profits (without the headaches). It's jam-packed with field-tested resources, including the email template I used to secure an endorsement from Tony Horton, detailed production timelines, guidelines for crafting a winning outline, software recommendations, tips for creating a professional design on a budget, and much more.

To reserve a free copy of *The Dawn of Books*, just go to www.jtev.me and join my mailing list. I've poured a lot of energy into this, and I know you're going to love it.

Cheers,

—J

Continue Your Journey

READ THE CONNECTION ALGORITHM

Do you want to continue your entrepreneurial journey by learning more about taking risks, defying the status quo, and living through passion? If so, consider checking out my other #1 bestselling book, *The Connection Algorithm*. It's a bit longer, but it's still a quick read. It covers more of my philosophy around becoming an entrepreneur, and explains why it's a worthy life choice.

You can always find my latest writings, links to my books, and other updates on my main website: www.jtev.me

BECOME PART OF THE STORY

If you want to contribute to this project, here are a few things you can do:

1. *Send me your story.* Are you thinking of jumping into an entrepreneurial journey? Are you currently in the middle of one? Already had a success? Did you hustle along the way? If you answered "yes" to any of

these questions, send me an email describing your experience. I might feature your story in future editions! Send an email with the subject line: "My Hustle Story" to jesse.tevelow@gmail.com.

2. *Share the book with your friends.* If you really enjoyed this, share it! You have the power to make this book fly, or fail. Sharing it on Twitter or Facebook can make all the difference in reaching a mainstream audience. I'd be forever grateful to you.

3. *Get in touch.* There are a few good ways to reach me. The first is my email: jesse.tevelow@gmail.com. I get a lot of email, so sometimes things slip by. Another option is Twitter. You can tweet at me @jtevelow and I'll probably see it.

4. *Leave your feedback.* If you're reading this in digital form, you'll be able to leave an Amazon review on the following screen. If you're reading a print copy, you can search the book title on Amazon.com and leave a review on the sales page. Reviews help people understand what the book is all about. I'd be incredibly appreciative if you gave me an honest star rating and left a few thoughts. Is something missing? What part

did you like best? How do you feel after reading it? Let me know. I read every single review. Reviews also show that the book is legitimate, and that people are actually reading it. So even if you don't have anything to say, but still want to give it a five star rating, I'll take it!

Tweet me @jtevelow
I'd love to hear from you!

Acknowledgments

I'd like to thank you, the reader. If you've gotten this far, I'm hoping *Hustle* had a positive impact on you. Never forget that you create your own reality. That power is yours, and yours alone. Enjoy your life, one moment at a time, and never stop moving.

I'd also like to thank my family, friends, and fans. Your support means the world to me. J

ABOUT THE AUTHOR

Jesse Warren Tevelow is an entrepreneur, health enthusiast, and writer. He's the #1 bestselling author of *The Connection Algorithm*, an original cofounder of PlayQ Inc., and an alumnus of TechStars. Jesse has been featured in various publications, including Businessweek Magazine, Forbes, *Do More Faster* (by Brad Feld and David Cohen), and *Upstarts* (by Donna Fenn). *Hustle* is Jesse's second book. To find out more, go to www.jtev.me